LIKE 'WHATAPLURRYMOBAOCKERS', SIR."

STOP LAUGHING, THIS IS SERIOUS!

STOP LAUGHING, THIS IS SERIOUS!

A social history of Australia in cartoons

Jonathan King

Cassell Australia

CASSELL AUSTRALIA LIMITED
44 Waterloo Rd, North Ryde, NSW 2113
30 Curzon Street, North Melbourne, Victoria 3051

First published 1978
Revised edition 1980
Edited by Irina Dunn
Set in 11/12, 12/13 Baskerville and 11/12 Helvetica by Modgraphic Pty Ltd, Adelaide
Produced by Graphic Consultants International, Singapore
F.980

National Library of Australia
Cataloguing in Publication Data
King, Jonathan Leslie, 1942-,
Stop laughing, this is serious.
ISBN 0 7269 4709 1. (Hardback)
ISBN 0 7269 4714 8. (Paperback)
1. Australia—History—1788-1978—Pictorial works. 2. Australia—Social conditions—1788-1978—Pictorial works. I. Title.
994

CONTENTS

OIL!

ACKNOWLEDGEMENTS

An illustrated book such as this can be compiled only with the help of a great number of people. The author wishes to thank the following libraries for their assistance in supplying cartoons and for their permission to reproduce them: British Museum, London, Department of Prints and Drawings; State Library of New South Wales, General Reference and Mitchell Libraries and Photographic Department; National Library of Australia and Rex Nan Kivell Collection, Canberra, cartoons from which appear in Chapter One; the La Trobe Library, Melbourne; State Library of South Australia, South Australian Collection, Adelaide; J. S. Battye Library of Western Australian History, Perth; State Library of Tasmania, Northern Regional Library, Launceston; and the State Library of Queensland, John Oxley Library, Brisbane.

The author also wishes to thank the following for granting permission to reproduce cartoons: Australian Consolidated Press (*Bulletin*); News Ltd (*Australian*, *Daily Mirror*, *Daily Telegraph*, *Truth*, *Adelaide News*); John Fairfax & Sons Ltd (*Sydney Morning Herald*, *Sun*, *Canberra Times*, *National Times*, *Financial Review*, *Sun-Herald*, *Smith's Weekly*); David Syme & Co Ltd (*Age*, *Sunday Press*); The Herald and Weekly Times Ltd (*Herald*, *Sun News Pictorial*, *Courier Mail*, Brisbane *Telegraph*, Adelaide *Advertiser*, *West Australian*, Perth *Daily News*, Hobart *Mercury*, *Northern Territory News*, *Australasian Post*); Incorporated Newsagencies Pty Ltd (*Nation Review*); the Communist Party of Australia (*Tribune*); and the Australian Workers' Union (*Australian Worker*). Every effort has been made to trace all copyright holders, but advice of any omissions would be appreciated.

Finally, particular thanks are due to the following: Ross Gibbs and the extremely flexible staff of the La Trobe Library which all but supplied an office and skeleton key that opened all vaults; Peter Leiss who patiently photographed all the cartoons except those in the first chapter and with Teddy's help printed them at a record-breaking pace; Andrew Webster who helped with selection and checked the copy for historical accuracy; Gail Sullivan who typed it cheerfully and professionally; Jeannie Mackintosh who selected cartoons; all those cartoonists who submitted their work; Irina Dunn who edited the manuscript; Kim Falkenmire who designed the layout; David Field who backed the project from start to finish; my father, John Essington King, who gathered many of the cartoons and provided great moral support; and my loyal wife Jane, for her invaluable advice and fine sense of humour.

Australia has long been recognized as the country with the world's most remarkable cartoonists. Whether this is a product of our rich, colourful history or merely our lazy predilection for pictures instead of words is open to question, but certainly a study of Australia's cartoonists from the early colonial newspaper artists to the contemporary cartoonist reveals a unique and entertaining view of Australian society.

A vast variation in style, approach, and readership appreciation is evident. The earliest works, whilst not cartoons, were aesthetic reflections on auspicious or infamous colonial matters—emigration, chain-gang convicts, gold-lust—forceful social and political comment, even then. In the 1880s the *Bulletin* succeeded in establishing our distinguished reputation for good cartoonists, who were beginning to thrive on the new-found freedom of the press and the emerging nationalism. The great names began to appear—Hop, Phil May and Norman Lindsay, and in 1911 came the immortal David Low. Their cartoons were beautifully illustrated, bitingly satirical, and often accompanied by paragraphs of written explanation which tended to drain a little of their spontaneity. Their approach epitomized the young Australian character, with its aggressive disregard for authority, contempt for the Establishment, and championship of the ordinary person. It was these qualities which the Australian reader came to look for in the cartoons and which set them so far above their dull overseas counterparts. They were rarely disappointed. Who could forget David Low's brilliant portrayal of Billy Hughes, or Norman Lindsay's koala bear faces gracing human politicians, or Hop's Little Boy from Manly?

These legendary names paved the way for the radically different approach of contemporary cartoonists. They are more entertaining, more succinct, and often more politically committed than their predecessors. Their style concentrates less on draftsmanship than on producing a good belly laugh to sharpen the political barb and get their point across.

FOREWORD

In the last ten years or so, cartoonists have had an abundance of material and personalities to supply their daily cartoon fodder. The election of the Labor government in 1972 produced a non-stop series of crises: dismissals, scandals, and social changes, climaxing with the constitutional crisis in November 1975 and the exit of Gough Whitlam in December 1977. Cartoonists were in their element, both with the events and faces of the era: Vincent Gair, the Irish leprechaun, Sir William McMahon, the political pixie, Al Grassby, the sartorial mouse, the many faces of Gough Whitlam, the supercilious rooster of the parliamentary farmyard, and the crumpled 'slept in' faces of Sir John Gorton and Don Chipp, to name just a few that gave the cartoonist joy.

The return of the Liberal government in 1975 saw an end to these turbulent times, and the passing on of many of the cartoonist's best-loved faces. Regardless of their political inclinations, modern cartoonists mourn their passing, for it seems that it will be many a year before such a wealth of material will come their way again. Meanwhile with the return to the status quo, cartoonists must once more concentrate on attacking the administration, for by the very nature of the job, they relegate themselves permanently to the Opposition benches.

Larry Pickering

Seen through the eyes of cartoonists, Australian history repeats itself. As if on a carousel, the same events come around and around again. Anybody who has lived long enough is able to confirm that the issues which preoccupy Australians today are variations of those that preoccupied their ancestors. Most of the great problems of today have been confronted by our grandparents, and if we can appreciate this and realize that *they* managed we may have more confidence in facing the great 'crises' of our own time.

Inflation, strikes and unemployment are recurring problems, with the last reaching shocking proportions in the 1840s, 1890s, 1930s and 1970s. Drinking has been an embarrassment from the rum-sodden start, and in fact was a far greater problem in the late eighteenth century, early 1900s and 1920s when six o'clock closing and prohibition were the controversial issues. Crimes of violence have disturbed previous generations, reaching peaks in the bushranging days of the 1860s and the gangster era of the 1920s. Allegations of police corruption are as old as the force itself and in Melbourne were more numerous in the early years of this century than they are even today.

Those worried by horrifying accidents such as the Granville train disaster or the collision between HMAS *Voyager* and HMAS *Melbourne* may be interested in the early cartoons portraying trains as 'coffin engines', cars as death traps and planes as evil spirits of the air. The collapse of the Westgate Bridge is in keeping with a long line of falling Melbourne bridges, and the subsequent delay on its rebuilding, as well as the lengthy construction of the Sydney eastern suburbs railway, is quite consistent with past performance.

Each generation has its own glamorous project that takes forever to build and ends up costing far too much. The Opera House took two decades and cost $100 million instead of an estimated $7 million, and the Sydney Harbour Bridge was several decades in the planning, designing and building.

Modern conservationists who believe that pollution is the greatest issue of our time may be interested to see the cartoons of the 1860s protesting

PREFACE

about the garbage-strewn beaches and around the turn of the century the sewer-spoilt Sydney surf.

Sport, too, has received its share of criticism, and the cartoons of the 1880s demonstrate how the sacred game of cricket was infiltrated by entrepreneurs as greedy as any today. Gambling has eroded the moral fibre of the community since the 1880s when the church launched anti-betting campaigns, just as it did during the Great War and the 1920s when the game of two-up had such a grip on the weekly paypacket. Every generation has had its terrible war, including the 1885 Sudan skirmish, the 1899 South African campaign, the Great War, World War II, Korea and Vietnam. Forgotten soldiers have invariably come home to an ungrateful country where unemployment and poverty made a mockery of the 'land fit for heroes' that they had been promised.

Each generation has fought its own disease including the smallpox, typhoid and cholera. epidemics of the 1870s and 1880s, the bubonic plague of the early 1900s, the influenza epidemic of the early 1920s, the polio of the 1930s and 1940s and the heart disease and cancer of the 1960s and 1970s. And finally, each generation of young men and women confront anew the ever-fascinating subject of relations between the sexes in a society that vacillates wildly between puritanism and permissiveness.

Resistance to change has been the one consistent theme. Like the traditional Luddites who opposed the introduction of the 'spinning jenny' in the textile mills of northern England in the late eighteenth century, Australians have almost invariably opposed any new development. The noisy, filthy and dangerous steam train was fought tooth and nail by the ancestors of the Citizens Against Freeways; the unpredictable horseless carriage and the aeroplane were both dismissed as passing fads. Gas and electricity were resisted by the grandparents of the members of the Movement Against Uranium Mining. Radio was mistrusted—especially the government propaganda voice: the ABC. Moving films and then 'talkies' were criticized for setting bad moral examples and increasing crime. Television was nicknamed 'Hellavision' because of the evils it threatened to bring into the home, and each new cult or musical fad from 'rock 'n' roll' to Beatlemania to punk rock has been condemned by both the forerunners and members of the Festival of Light.

The picture presented by the cartoonists is frank and incisive. There is no cover-up; it is history as it really was. The material was selected from a wide range of mainstream journals and newspapers. It is organized chronologically and divided into historically distinct periods. The major preoccupations of each generation are recalled; often they echo themes of earlier times. An attempt has been made to portray the developing Australian identity, and each generation can be represented by a particular character which personifies the spirit of the age. The changing fashions are also recorded at the end of each chapter, as is the march towards nudity.

Although this social history stands on its own it is also a companion volume to *The Other Side of the Coin: a Cartoon History of Australia* (Cassell, 1976), which emphasizes Australia's political development. Great effort has been made to represent the major cartoonists of Australia, past and present. However, because the country has such a fine tradition and even something of an international lead in cartooning, it has not always been possible to do justice to them all. The final chapter displays at least one cartoon from each of the forty major cartoonists working on mainstream publications today. The publication, year of cartoon and the artist are given where possible.

If *the past is prologue* then perhaps these cartoons can provide insights into the future—or at least into how Australians as a whole will respond to developments over the horizon; and thus we may learn lessons from our forgotten forebears. There will, inevitably, be times when we *Stop Laughing* and realize *This Is Serious.*

Jonathan King
October 1978

CHAPTER I
Farewell to Old England Forever 1776–1809

Let Them Eat Cake
Life at the Bottom
In My Lady's Chamber
Rounding Up the Convicts
Fancy Fashions: What Next?

CHAPTER I
Farewell to Old England Forever 1776–1809

MY POLL & MY PARTNER JOE

The first Australians

LATEST INTELLIGENCE.

Latest news from England

The age in which Botany Bay was born could have been designed expressly for social cartoonists, for almost daily there was something new upon which to comment. Europe was changing so rapidly that nothing appeared too sacred to attack. The rising of the new order from the ashes of the old was accompanied by warfare, violence and destruction. The social and political upheavals of the day are reflected in the art of the period. English cartoonists ridiculed the Church, the Crown, the aristocracy, lawyers, military officers, and anyone else who caught their eye. They had plenty of raw material to draw upon. Across the Atlantic, the American colonies wrested independence from 'mad' King George III to lay the foundations of what was to become the most powerful and wealthiest nation in modern times. Thirteen years later, in 1789, the old order in Europe was finally buried when the French overthrew the monarchy and proclaimed a republic in the name of 'liberty, equality and fraternity'.

Meanwhile, another 'revolution' was under way in Britain—the industrial revolution, which created in its wake its own share of turmoil and bloodshed as thousands were displaced from their traditional employment. This and the Enclosure Acts drove many people to the cities where they faced high prices, uncertain employment and appalling conditions. Oppression, poverty, drunkenness and disease were symptoms of their problem and drove many to a life of crime. Theirs were the ranks from which many convicts came, and theirs was the lot that was portrayed time and again by contemporary cartoonists, of whom Hogarth (1697–1764) was the precursor. In transforming the cartoon from an aristocratic diversion to a broader vehicle for social criticism, Hogarth established a tradition that was eventually to lead to the creation of the cheeky, irreverent and bawdy cartoons that appeared in that arch social satirist, *Punch* (1841).

Not only were there political upheavals during this period, but religious and moral codes were also being overturned. In both America and France, religious orders were dissolved and Acts were passed freeing people from the dictates of the Church. The introduction of civil marriage and divorce in the new republics had such an impact that the Toleration Acts relaxing religious laws in Britain soon followed. Many took advantage of the new mood of secularism, not least the cartoonists, who satirized the many vices of their society.

It was against this background that the penal colony which became Australia was established. The loss of its American colonies in 1776 had forced Britain to find another repository for its unwanted criminals, and New South Wales was chosen on the advice of James Matra, a seaman who had travelled with Captain Cook to Botany Bay in 1770. In 1788, the First Fleet to New South Wales carried 750 convicts. The second, arriving in 1790, brought 1 200, and the third brought 1 880 more the following year. Although the first free settlers came out in 1793, they did not outnumber convicts until many years later. Finding little to recommend the colony when he arrived in 1810, Governor Macquarie set about reforming the prison outpost that had served little purpose but to transplant the worst of London's social problems to a remote country.

Colonial comment on this state of affairs was sparse in the early years. There were few local publications in New South Wales for the first fifty years; British newspapers kept the penal colony informed of world affairs—although somewhat belatedly—and British humour kept the colonies amused. Certainly there was no regular resident cartoonist until *Melbourne Punch* was established in 1855.

Thus we rely on British cartoonists to give us a portrait of the age, and James Gillray (1757–1815) was one of the most brilliant. His cartoons dominate this chapter. Gillray suffered a repressed childhood in Chelsea, and his reaction to this repression is reflected in the daring of his work, in which all the sacred cows of the period are held up to ridicule. An obituary notice said of him: 'He did not seek to conceal his poisonous draughts in a gilded cup. He lived like a caterpillar on the green leaf of reputation.' Like most artists of the day, he sold his work on cards in publishers' shop-front windows, and, according to one witness, 'the enthusiasm is indescribable when the next drawing appears; it is veritable madness. You have to make your way in through the crowd with your fists'.

Cartoonists such as Gillray recorded the character of the society that gave birth to Botany Bay and then continued to influence the colonial outpost for many decades, even though the convicts had bidden *Farewell To Old England Forever.*

Free passage to the colonies

1751–1806
Let Them Eat Cake

The industrial revolution may have given Britain an international lead in production but the people paid a high price. Thousands lost their jobs through the invention of machines which made their traditional crafts redundant. These displaced people travelled the country in search of work, cutting family ties that were centuries old. Many drifted into London where, by 1810, the population had reached one million. Here they faced high taxes, filthy slums and unhygienic sewerage, social injustice, drink and disease. Circumstances drove many to crime and then, when they were caught, British justice propelled them first to the American colonies and, from 1788, to New South Wales.

1 *The 'Friend of the People' and his Petty-New-Tax-Gatherer, paying John Bull a visit* (Gillray, 1806). Crippling taxation in London ruined many householders, whose meagre earnings were eroded by the vast array of taxes imposed by the government to finance expensive wars and other public programmes.

2 *Substitutes for Bread; or Right Honorables Saving the Loaves & Dividing the Fishes* (Gillray, 1795). The social inequalities of the day were exacerbated during a time of pending famine by a call from the privileged classes for the poor to find substitutes for bread. Petitions from the 'starving swine' outside beg for 'crumbs which drop from your table'.

3 *Gin Lane* (Hogarth, 1751). Alcoholism wreaked havoc in the slums of London where the gin trade thrived. Probably of a poor quality, the drink was cheap and carried the popular guarantee, 'Drunk for a penny, Dead drunk for tuppence'.

4 *Un petit Souper à la Parisienne or A Family of Sans-Culottes refreshing, after the fatigues of the day* (Gillray, 1792). If social conditions were bad in Britain they were shocking in post-revolutionary France. Food shortages were so great and the price of bread so high that, according to popular legend, Parisians turned to cannibalism to fill their empty stomachs.

1

2

3

4

1796–1802
Life at the Bottom

With the almost non-existent hygiene of the period the state of public health was shocking. The only provisions for sewage were open gutters and streams; few public fountains contained water fit to drink; and germs thrived in the filth of London. Smallpox and gout were among the more common diseases. Great efforts, therefore, were made to find cures to alleviate the sickness and suffering, but when they were discovered, their effect was often either mistrusted or misunderstood.

1 *The Cow-Pock or the Wonderful Effects of the New Inoculation* (Gillray, 1802). Edward Jenner's invention in 1796 of a vaccination to cure smallpox was strongly resisted. Although the injection of a small dose of cow-pox bred an immunity to the disease, many imagined that the vaccination would accelerate it.

2 *Punch cures the Gout, the Colic and the 'Tisick* (Gillray, 1799). In the murky world of medical practice it was an inducement to be sick when the cure was so attractive. The blending of wine or spirits with hot water or milk and the addition of lemons or spice created the magic cure-all punch, which was also an irresistible intoxicant.

3 *The Gout* (Gillray, 1799). Caused by a dysfunctioning in the body's ability to break down proteins, gout produced severe swelling of the joints and painful inflammation, especially around the big toe. For thousands it added to life's miseries until, many generations later, a treatment was devised to counter the over-production of uric acid.

4 *National Conveniences* (Gillray, 1796). The cause of many diseases of the period was the unhygienic and primitive sewerage. A modern sewerage system was not installed in London until the 1860s, when Louis Pasteur developed his germ theory of disease and Joseph Lister started practising antiseptic surgery.

1

2

3

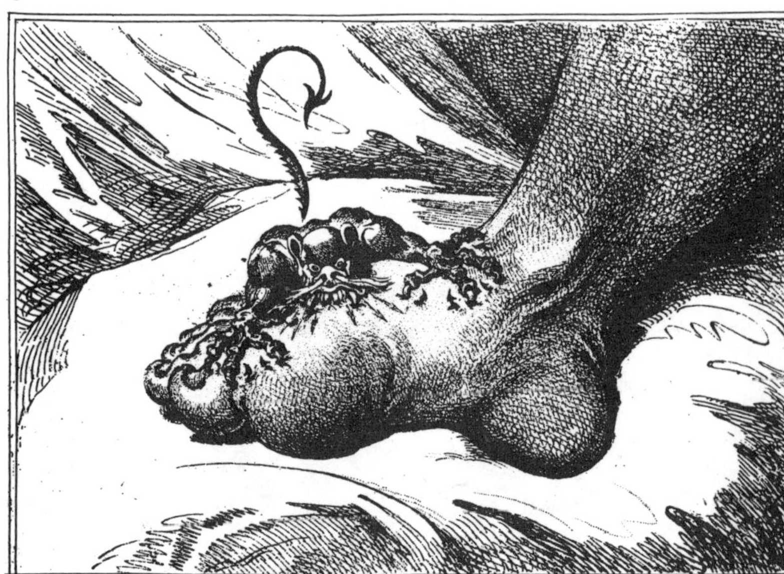

English Convenience – the Water Closet.

Scotch Convenience, – the Bucket.

French Convenience, – le Commodites.

Dutch Convenience. – the Lake.

NATIONAL CONVENIENCES.

1751–1800
In My Lady's Chamber

Conventional morality was overturned and a new ribald code ushered in following the rebellions and industrial turmoils of the age. With the dissolution of religious orders and the introduction of civil marriage and divorce in France in 1792, it must have seemed to many pious Christians that the Church had been overthrown by the Devil. Toleration Acts were passed in Britain in response to this new mood of secularism that was sweeping the continent.

1 *The Monster going to take his Afternoons Luncheon* (Gillray, 1790). The licentiousness of the day is satirized in this portrayal of the voracious sexual 'monster'.

2 *The Man of Feeling in search of Indispensibles—A Scene at the Little French Milleners* (Gillray, 1800). A voyeur attempts to resolve the puzzle of the day—were the newly invented pockets in ladies' underwear located near the ankle or in a 'more eligible situation'?

3 *Fashionable Contrasts, or The Duchess's little Shoe yielding to the Magnitude of the Duke's Foot* (Gillray, 1791). The popularity of such daring cartoons as this reflects something of the permissiveness that prevailed at the time.

4 *An emblematic print on the South Sea* (Hogarth, 1751). Eighteenth-century London—the centre from which many convicts were committed—is portrayed here as the city of the Devil. Churchmen gamble for money (bottom left), while ladies of fashion climb stairs to hire a husband and prostitutes advertise for a 'ride' on a merry-go-round.

5 *'Oh! that this too too solid flesh would melt'* (Gillray, 1791). The rich of the age encountered problems no less frustrating than those faced by Hamlet. These included obesity which, apart from hindering the course of true love, made life extremely uncomfortable for those who had overindulged.

1

2

3

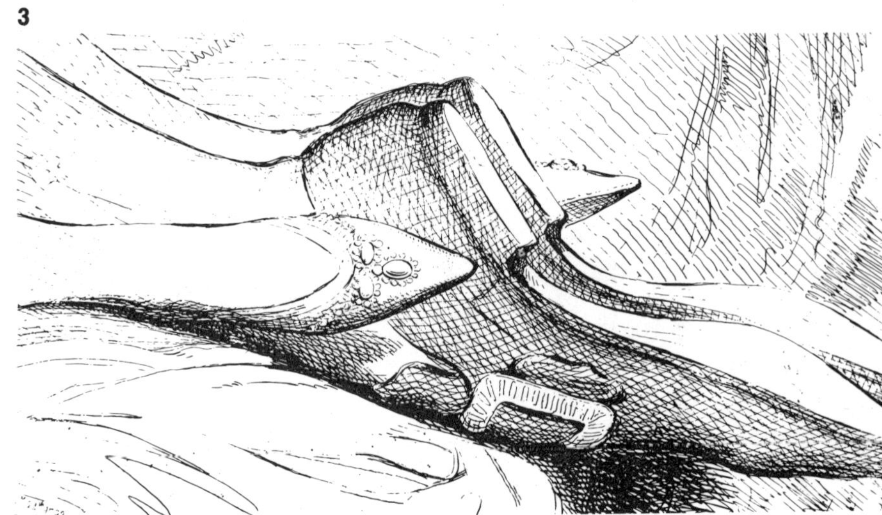

4

5

"Oh! that this too too solid flesh would melt."

1786–1810 Rounding Up the Convicts

Although the majority of convicts sent to New South Wales were professional criminals with previous convictions, the society from which they were derived certainly did not provide models of moral rectitude and Christian principles. With a corrupt Church, a dishonest legal profession and a hypocritical set of laws, poor prisoners stood little chance in their battle against the authorities. The establishment of the penal colony on the other side of the globe was a convenient way of getting rid of the unwanted criminals.

1 *Vices overlook'd in the New Proclamation* (Gillray, 1792). The hypocrisy of laws which forbade the dangerous vices of 'Thinking, Speaking & Writing' yet allowed 'Avarice, Drunkenness, Gambling and Debauchery, riled cartoonists.
2 *The First Day of Term, or The Devil among the Lawyers* (Bowles, 1786). Bribery and corruption were common in the courts, and prisoners without money had little chance of being acquitted. Here the barristers fight for the lucrative cases being handed out by the Devil.
3 *St. George's Volunteers Charging down Bond Street, after clearing the Ring in Hyde Park, & Storming the Dunghill at Marybone* (Gillray, 1797). The behaviour of the military forces left much to be desired.
4 *He steers his flight Aloft, incumbent on the dusky air That felt unusual weight* (Gillray, 1810). The fire balloon that had flown people over the English Channel in 1785 is here powered by the hot air promises of the Prince of Wales, who sided with the Roman Catholics in their struggle against Protestant denominations in England.
5 *Destruction of the French Collossus* (Gillray, 1798). The wickedness of post-revolutionary France sent a wave of shock through Europe and the British Empire. Clutching the guillotine and treading on the Holy Bible, the monstrous French colossus is struck down even as it spans the Mediterranean.

1

2

3

183
down Bond Street
S.t GEORGE'S-VOLUNTEERS Charging the FRENCH, after clearing the Ring in Hyde Park, & Storming the Dunghill at Marybone.

4

— Tentanda via est qua me quoque possim
Tollere humo —
— He steers his flight
Aloft, incumbent on the dusky air
That felt unusual weight

5

Destruction of the French Collossus.
"Shall the Works of a wicked Nation remain? – shall the Monuments of Oppression not be destroyed? — shall the
"Lightning not blast the Image which the Destroyers have set up against the God of Heaven, & against his Laws?"

1795–1810
Fancy Fashions: What Next?

Only the wealthy could indulge in the extravagance of contemporary fashion, which provided the rest of the populace with an amusing distraction, and cartoonists with an unending topic for satire. There was the neo-classical revival of muslin gowns with their provocative slashes, the absurdity of the plume, tall boots for men and the ultimate affectation of the padded shoulders. And this is not to mention that scandalous new dance—the waltz.

1 *Ladies Dress, as it soon will be* (Gillray, 1796). The requirement that fashionable dress be a display both of finery and of flesh was met in this lady's apparel.

2 *La Walse, Le Bon Genre* (Gillray, 1810). The waltz was introduced to English ballrooms in 1810 and caused a sensation that rippled through society for many years before the avant-garde dance was eventually accepted.

3 *'Monstrosities' of 1799—Scene Kensington Gardens* (Gillray, 1799). As the century turned, the fashionable set vied with each other until they created 'imaginary monsters of outrageous appearance'.

4 *'And catch the living Manners as they rise'* (Gillray, 1795). To cartoonists with a social conscience the affectations of the age epitomized decadence, and underlined the mindless extravagance that seemed to fly in the face of the less fortunate.

5 *A Pair of Polished Gentlemen* (Gillray, 1801). Taking their lead from the flamboyant Prince of Wales, the fashionable gentlemen of the age never travelled without their dashing boots. A challenge is here issued when one of the gentlemen kicks over the mandatory bottle of 'Royal Blacking'.

1

2

※ "MONSTROSITIES" of 1799,- Scene Kensington Gardens.

4

"And catch the living Manners as they rise.

5

A Pair of POLISHED Gentlemen

CHAPTER II

Bound Down by Iron Chains 1810–1868

The Arrival of Our Forebears
Met by Pests
All Roads Lead to Ruin
Our Model Omnibus
Marvellous Smelbourne
Celestial Delicacies
The Work of the Devil
Domestic Bliss Downunder
From Criminal to Cosmopolitan
Fancy Fashions: What Next?

CHAPTER II

Bound Down by Iron Chains 1810–1868

Bound down by iron chains

If the events of the late eighteenth century had stimulated cartoonists, those of the first half of the nineteenth century gave them unlimited scope. With the transformation of the world taking place before their very eyes the successors of Hogarth and Gillray developed their art to a high degree.

The violence of the earlier period may have passed, but there was never any shortage of material. The defeat of Napoleon ushered in an era of peace, and the accession of the young Victoria to the throne in 1837 restored a respectability to the monarchy that had been eroded by her predecessors, George III and George IV. In European countries, people's uprisings in 1831 and 1848 forced the introduction of better working conditions, but the more stable Britain pursued the path of reformism rather than revolution. Slavery throughout the British Empire was abolished in 1834 and the conditions of working people were much improved through the efforts of individuals such as Robert Owen.

As an outpost of the British Empire, life in the Australian colonies was directly affected by the social and technological innovations that were changing the character of the old world. In 1831, government-assisted immigration to New South Wales was initiated, and two years later, free settlers outnumbered convicts for the first time. The free settlers were able to form themselves into a strong domestic lobby and, together with British reformers and the London-based Molesworth Committee, were successful in having transportation to New South Wales abolished in 1840, although it continued to Western Australia until 1868. All in all, the colonies had received 168 000 convicts, amongst whom were a number of the Tolpuddle 'martyrs', transported in 1834 for attempting to form a trade union.

A social revolution was taking place and there was, in Britain, talk about universal education. Although the Churches may have vied for control over the new education—especially in the Australian colonies, where Catholic and Protestant forces competed fiercely—education itself was weakening the influence of religion, not least of all through the impact of Karl Marx and Charles Darwin.

The rising material expectations of the populace

coincided with an extraordinary explosion of scientific achievement that changed the face of the Empire and its colonies, much to the delight of the cartoonists, who satirized each new development as it was introduced. This was the generation that switched from sail to steam, from wood to iron, from horse to locomotive, from sea mail to telegraph. Suddenly, journeying to the colonies made more sense.

British newspapers imported with English migrants provide us with much of our record of the age, since there were few local publications for the first fifty years. *Punch* (or, *The London Charivari* as it was first named, after Charles Philipon's French magazine) was founded in 1841. Imitating the style of their British counterpart, the *Melbourne Punch* (1855) and the *Sydney Punch* (1864) held a satirical mirror to the colonies, mercilessly lampooning their bungling attempts to adapt British customs and overseas inventions to life 'down under'. Two of the earliest colonial imitators were Nicholas Chevalier, a Swiss artist who worked for the Melbourne paper, and an English caricaturist, Montague Scott, who was based in Sydney. Having come to the antipodes not in chains but in search of gold, they both found in the expanding colonies a rich source of humour waiting to be mined. The original penal settlement had evolved from the central Sydney Cove establishment to the six flourishing towns that were to become the State capitals of the future. The construction of new buildings, roads, railways, bridges, schools, water systems, banks and hospitals in the colony provided cartoonists with unlimited raw material, for not only did the innovations arrive in the colonies long after their adoption in Europe and Britain, but when they were developed locally, they almost invariably went wrong.

By the end of this period, Australian cartooning had developed a distinctly indigenous idiom, its foundations resting firmly in the peculiar social conditions of the country—its convict origins, the settlers' struggles in a harsh climate, the growing pains of a developing national consciousness, and an attempt to live down the recent past, when the majority had been *Bound Down By Iron Chains*.

Convict class

1816–1817
The Arrival of Our Forebears

When Governor Macquarie assumed control in 1810 the character of the penal colony was overwhelmingly criminal. The three fleets brought a total of 3 830 convicts, and from 1793 to 1810 an average of 400 a year arrived. By 1815 approximately 1 000 were being transported every year, the number peaking at an average of 5 000 a year between 1826 and 1835. After this, the numbers gradually declined as transportation was successively abolished in different colonies, ending in Western Australia in 1868. The colonies expanded rapidly with a huge increase in the population following the discovery of gold in 1851. This stimulated the improvement of roads and vehicles connecting mining sites with large towns, although travel anywhere within the colonies was still fairly hazardous, as many contemporary cartoons show.

1 *Arms of the Greeks* (Cruikshank, 1817). The gamble of life was such that those who were sentenced had little choice between transportation to Botany Bay or being hanged and sent to Hell. Many preferred death to Hell on earth at Botany Bay.

2 *What a Prime Prig I am my Boys* (Marks, 1816). Actors who set bad examples by 'stealing' on stage were blamed for the downfall of some convicts, who were sent to New South Wales on the ships in the background.

3 *Distant View—a promising actor* (Cruikshank, 1817). Most of the convicts were transported for stealing. Here, with a transport waiting complete with Botany Bay flag, a ragged youth commits a crime that will earn him between seven and fourteen years' exile.

4 *The Landing of Our Forefathers from an old print* (Hop, *Bulletin*, 1891). A satirical recreation more than a century later of the landing of convicts at Sydney Cove in 1788. Dissatisfied with Botany Bay, Governor Phillip moved the fleet to Port Jackson where a formal possession ceremony was enacted on 26 January.

1

2

3

Distant View – a promising actor

4

1830–1856
Met by Pests

For both the convicts and those free immigrants who were to follow them from 1793 onwards, one of the major discomforts in the new colony were pests. Unlike the 'green and pleasant land' they had left behind, immigrants found a wide brown land that was full of flies, bugs, spiders, rats, mosquitoes and snakes. In the water the situation was not much better, for alligators and sharks awaited the unwary. On top of this was the heat. Many of the British 'arrivals' became subsequent 'departures' because of the seeming hostility of the country, which broke the spirit of all but the most resilient.

1 *Flourishing State Of The Swan River Thing* (Seymour, 1830). A cartoonist's portrayal of a free settler family one year after the founding of the colony in Western Australia. Conditions were so tough at Perth that settlers requested convicts in 1850, ten years after the abolition of transportation to New South Wales.

2 *How Alligators Are Caught In Queensland* (Hop, *Bulletin*, 1888). A later, southerner's joke about the 'deep north' claimed that sugar planters used their family as bait to attract alligators for their table.

3 *Just Confidence* (*Melbourne Punch*, 1856). The shark was feared from the start. Here a 'Stout party' in Port Phillip Bay says, 'Sharks, man! Nonsense! All a fable! Why don't they come and bite me? Do you think they wouldn't if there were any. But there isn't such a thing in the Ba . . .' (interruption and sensation).

4 *Involuntary Investigations Into An Australian History* (*Melbourne Punch*, 1856). An imaginary first night in the colonies, before the days of flywire and other protective barriers.

1

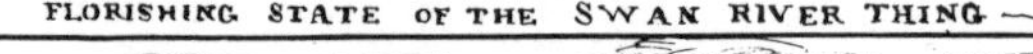

2

HOW ALLIGATORS ARE CAUGHT IN QUEENSLAND.

3

JUST CONFIDENCE.

INVOLUNTARY INVESTIGATIONS INTO AN AUSTRALIAN HISTORY.

I.

This is Mr. FORTEWINCK's first night in Australia. He had no idea that he should find things so comfortable.

II.

He has not been very long in bed however, before he finds it necessary to get up again. A terrible slaughter ensues.

III.

Mr. FORTEWINCK sees a Tarantula for the first time, and is more struck by it's size than it's beauty.

IV.

Confound the rats!

V.

Mr. FORTEWINCK resolves to go to bed no more, and covering his head with a handkerchief to keep off the musquitos, (which begin to be troublesome), he waits for morning.

VI.

When he studies his appearance in the glass, and identifies himself with difficulty.

1855–1865
All Roads Lead to Ruin

The MacAdam method of constructing new roads from broken stones may have been pioneered in 1815 in the 'old country' but it was many years before roads in the colonies gained respectable surfaces. Initially the going was so rough on land that river transport prevailed and the Hawkesbury, Yarra and other rivers were the principal highways of the age. Governor Macquarie initiated many public works that included a far-reaching programme of road building from 1813. But with the growth of the colonies following the discovery of gold in 1851, the roads were never quite able to keep pace with the greatly increased traffic and inevitably became a prime target for satire.

1 *A Sketch from the Album of F. Murphy, Esq.* (Chevalier, *Melbourne Punch*, 1857). Waiting ladies crouch under umbrellas in the driving rain as their menfolk urge the horses across a ford made impassable by wet weather.

2 *A Substantial Man In Difficulties* (Chevalier, *Melbourne Punch*, 1865). Crossing roads before they were sealed was never straightforward, and wet weather in particular created many pitfalls.

3 *The Roads. The High Road By Bakery Hill* (*Melbourne Punch*, 1856). Although perhaps never quite as bad as this, the condition of the roads in the colonies was certainly a favourite target for satirical cartoons.

4 *Mr. Punch Pays A Visit To The Diggings* (Chevalier, *Melbourne Punch*, 1855). If the roads were bad in the main centres of civilization, on the diggings they barely existed.

1

MELBOURNE PUNCH'S ALMANACK FOR 1857.

A Sketch from the Album of F. Murphy, Esq.

2

A SUBSTANTIAL MAN IN DIFFICULTIES.
SCENE *A Leading Business Thoroughfare in Melbourne.*

3

THE ROADS.
THE HIGH ROAD BY BAKERY HILL.

4

MR. PUNCH PAYS A VISIT TO THE DIGGINGS.

1856–1865
Our Model Omnibus

Horse-drawn omnibuses were pioneered in 1829 in London, but in the colonies, where the new MacAdam style roads were known by reputation only, it was some time before they were introduced. The influx of people during the 1850s justified their services no matter how rough the roads, and before long omnibuses were in use in most of the larger towns. Many of the public services, including transport, the fire brigade and the post office, had been strained by the sudden population growth and became the butt of much cartooning humour.

1 *The Pitt Street Juggernaut, Or What* may *Happen With The Tram* (Mason, *Sydney Bulletin*, 1865). A hansom cab and a cart are overturned as an imaginary tram ploughs through the crowded streets of Sydney.

2 *A St. Kilda Omnibus On Sunday* (Grosse, *Melbourne Punch*, 1865). The public transport facilities, strained at the best of times, were overloaded during weekends when members of the public took popular Sunday drives such as that to St Kilda Beach.

3 *Wonders Will Never Cease* (*Melbourne Punch*, 1860). The arrival of the crinoline did little to ease the problem of space shortage on public transport.

4 *Fire! Fire! Fire!* (*Melbourne Punch*, 1856). Wood fires, candlelight and widespread pipesmoking played havoc with the timber cottages of the early colonists. Although fires were an everyday occurrence, the performance of the brigade left much to be desired.

5 *Outside And Inside or A Private Post Office At The Diggings* (*Melbourne Punch*, 1856). When the postal service remained in small private hands, it rarely met the needs of the swelling population, especially on the diggings.

1

THE PITT STREET JUGGERNAUT,
OR WHAT *may* HAPPEN WITH THE TRAM.

2

A ST. KILDA OMNIBUS ON SUNDAY.
Conductor.—"JUMP UP SIR—LOTS O' ROOM."

3

WONDERS WILL NEVER CEASE.
THESE CONVEYANCES ARE LICENSED TO CARRY SIX, AND HAVE BEEN KNOWN TO CONTAIN SEVEN; BUT HOW THEY MANAGE IT, GOODNESS ONLY KNOWS.

4

FIRE! FIRE! FIRE!

The Fire Bell has roused all Melbourne, in the middle of the night, and the water-carts and engines arrive at Mr. Smith's just in time to **prevent the fire in his back** kitchen chimney from going out by itself.

5

OUTSIDE AND INSIDE.

OR

A PRIVATE POST OFFICE AT THE DIGGINGS.

1860–1884
Marvellous Smelbourne

By the 1880s the open sewers, rotting rubbish dumps and general filth of the town had earned Melbourne the nickname 'Smelbourne'. The population had grown as a result of the gold rushes, associated industries and the land boom but the public services had not developed to cope with the sudden pressures of a growing city. Outbreaks of disease—particularly typhoid and cholera—were common, as the drinking water was often contaminated by the sewerage system. The Sydney water supply was no healthier.

1 *Dirt And Disease* (*Melbourne Punch*, 1884). Even in the 'Model Boroughs' of Melbourne the smell was so bad that the 'commuter' had to hold his nose most of the way home from the city and also risk disease from the rotting garbage in his path.

2 *Design* (*Melbourne Punch*, 1860). To drink from the public water was to sign your own death warrant, according to the popular belief of the day. Contaminated water carried typhoid and cholera germs, and the fountains on the Yan Yean system delivered water discoloured by sewage.

3 *The Water: Cure Or Kill?* (Scott, *Sydney Punch*, 1873). Scott, the cartoonist, was among those who campaigned to have Sydney's deadly water supply purified once it was shown that the outbreak of cholera and typhoid had been caused by water that doctors were giving to the sick.

4 *The Delightful Climate Of Australia* (*Melbourne Punch*, 1865). Dust storms, wind and rain made life extremely unpleasant for pedestrians before the roads were sealed.

1

DIRT AND DISEASE.

WHAT THE SOUTH MELBOURNE CITIZEN OF THE PERIOD HAS TO WADE THROUGH NIGHTLY ON HIS JOURNEY HOME FROM BUSINESS TO HIS RESIDENCE IN THE "MODEL BOROUGH."

2

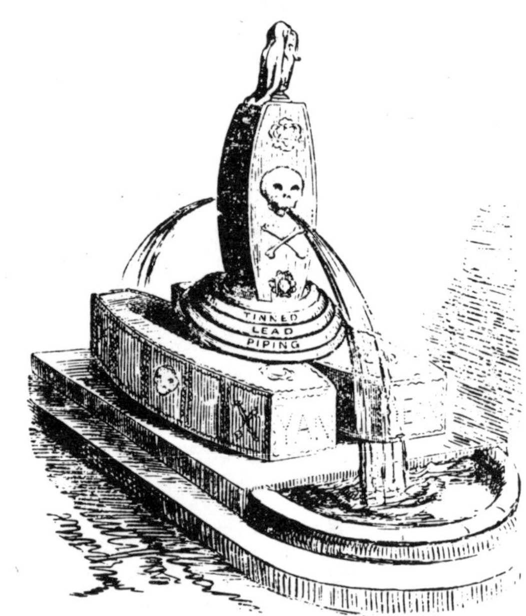

DESIGN

For a street fountain to disseminate the blessings of our wholesom and refreshing water-supply.

3

THE WATER CURE—OR KILL?

THE DELIGHTFUL CLIMATE OF AUSTRALIA.

I.
An eminent Melbourne Merchant (resident in the Toorak Road), resolves to walk into Town this delightful morning.

II.
Before he reaches the St. Kilda road, he is unfortunately overtaken by a slight dust storm.

III.
Bountiful Nature, however, soon relieves him with a change of weather.

IV.
The Eminent Melbourne Merchant reaches his Counting House,

1857–1876
Celestial Delicacies

Apart from the racial and employment threats posed by the Chinese who arrived with the gold rushes, there were many strange and frightening customs associated with these 'oriental gentlemen'. Little was known about them or their ways and in the absence of real contact, prejudice inspired many stories of pure fantasy. These provoked further prejudice and inspired the anti-Chinese restrictive legislation which checked their influx from 1855 onwards.

1 *The Slave Trade In Victoria* (*Touchstone*, 1870). One of the things that white Australians have always feared is the contamination of their racial 'purity'. It was rumoured that lonely Chinese men offered large sums of money to the mothers of attractive daughters in a form of 'slave trading'.

2 *A Celestial Delicacy* (Chevalier, *Melbourne Punch*, 1865). A favourite story concerned the Chinese liking for cats. Here the customer asks, 'I soy; how much you cook him for—that one Cat?' 'Cook the Cat, Sir!!' the shop assistant replies. 'Yas, you sabbee? Roast em Cat—me eat em Cat—vary good'. To which the shop assistant responds, 'Lawk, Sir: The Cat aint to be heaten. (Aside)—Did hever hany one see sich Cannibal Inguns'.

3 *Revival Of The Fine Old Australian Sport Of License—Hunting* (*Melbourne Punch*, 1857). Hated by many diggers because they accumulated wealth by fossicking through the discarded earth for tiny traces of gold, the Chinese were often persecuted on the goldfields.

4 *Celestial Happiness* (Chevalier, *Melbourne Punch*, 1865). An image that symbolizes the deep-rooted fears about the consequences of Chinese immigration to Australia.

5 *Celestiality; or, Truth stranger than Fiction* (Scott, *Sydney Punch*, 1876). A report by Mr Punch on the Common Lodging Houses of Sydney described the grip of opium as a 'Leprosy' and portrayed the Chinese as seducers of Australian women.

1

THE SLAVE TRADE IN VICTORIA. A right proper field for the champions of morality. Christian mothers selling their daughters to the Chinese.

2

A CELESTIAL DELICACY.

3

REVIVAL OF THE FINE OLD AUSTRALIAN SPORT OF LICENSE-HUNTING.

"Up here all of us, and especially our jurymen, are looking forward with great pleasure to the prospect of a good Chinese hunting season. Under the proposed new law the sport will gain much extra *eclat*, by being carried on with official sanction and patronage, and not as hitherto, merely by sufferance. I send you an anticipatory sketch by a local artist."
(Extract from private letter from Beechworth.)

4

5

Celestiality; or, Truth stranger than Fiction.

1856–1888
The Work of the Devil

Excessive drinking was a problem in the colonies from the very beginning. On his arrival in 1800, the incoming governor, Phillip Gidley King, observed, 'There are only two classes of people in the colony, the rum sellers and the rum drinkers'. Rum, in fact, served as a currency for some time and, once established as the main form of social diversion in the penal colony, took many years to control. Few people were free of the grip of the bottle, which at times corrupted the Church as well, even in its missionary role and despite the formation of numerous temperance movements.

1 *A Missionary Society Report—Somewhat Condensed* (May, *Bulletin*, 1888). A colonial attack on the British Churches, which are here personified as an 'angelic' John Bull bringing the blessings of civilization—'demoralization, war and ruin'—to Islanders off the Queensland coast.

2 *The Conversion Of The Aborigines* (*Melbourne Punch*, 1857). With a bottle in one hand and the Bible in the other, the missionary of the colonies—complete with pipe in belt—brings 'enlightenment' to the natives.

3 *Popular Beverages* (*Melbourne Punch*, 1860). A racist joke which puns on the Aboriginal word for 'woman'.

4 *A Brave Resolve* (*Melbourne Punch*, 1865). The habit of smoking had by no means become widespread and it was considered poor taste to smoke in public.

5 *Evening Service* (*Melbourne Punch*, 1856). Drinking became so popular in the colonies that pressures were exerted to open public houses on Sunday. Many thought it would be better than the hypocrisy of the sly-grog shop which was often 'protected' by the law.

1

2

THE CONVERSION OF THE ABORIGINES.

3

POPULAR BEVERAGES.
Gin and Water.

4

A BRAVE RESOLVE.

FAIR COUSIN: You don't mean to say you're going to smoke, Charles, and there are strangers in the carriage?

CHARLES: Well, as I don't see any gentlemen among 'em to kick up a row, I think I may as well take a whiff.

5

EVENING SERVICE.

[SCENE—*The Pig and Whistle*, —— *Street, Melbourne*. TIME—*Sunday evening*.]

DISTINGUISHED PHILANTHROPIST: Constable, I fear liquor is being sold in this establishment to-night.

POLICEMAN: Liquor, Sir; bless your 'art, Sir, no. Werry serious landlord here, Sir. Always has a prayer meetin' o' Sundays, and they're now a singin' o' hymns.

(*Moral*.—Never alter a law which works so well as that which now keeps the public houses closed on Sunday).

1854–1865
Domestic Bliss Down Under

Life on the home front was fraught with difficulties for the early settlers who had few of the comforts of their European counterparts and often not even a home to call their own. Traditional social customs were difficult to preserve in temporary settlements such as the diggings. The criminal element in the early community threatened householders who had possessions, and the absence of labour-saving devices made life a continual struggle. The invention of the first dishwasher and carpet sweeper in 1865 promised to ease the load. However, it was many years before these appliances reached the colonies, and when they did they were too expensive for most families.

1 *Domestic Machinery* (*Melbourne Punch*, 1865). The invention of the dishwasher in 1865 occasioned many satirical cartoons, especially against servants who were prone to throwing everything but the kitchen sink into the new device.

2 *The Nocturnal Adventures of Mr. Jones* (*Melbourne Punch*, 1857). With so many convicts in the colonies, pardoned or otherwise, it was not surprising that burglaries were a common occurrence. Here, the weakness of the robbers for grog and gambling gives them away.

3 *Domestic Bliss In Australia* (Calvert, *Melbourne Punch*, 1857). This satirical jibe is directed at the diggers who spend yet another sleepless night under 'waterproof' canvas as a consequence of being gulled by advertizing.

4 *Topsy Turvey, or, our Antipodes* (Leech, *London Punch*, 1854). A British view of Regent Street, down under, where gold discoveries had enriched the common people and placed them above the professional classes who here wait on the uncouth but wealthy working classes.

1

DOMESTIC MACHINERY.

LADY OF ENGINEERING TALENT IS SUPPOSED TO HAVE PROVIDED HER SERVANT WITH A WASHING APPARATUS. DIRTY ADVANTAGE THEREOF APPEARS TO HAVE BEEN TAKEN.

2

Mr. JONES hears a Cat in the Parlour, and entertains a fell design.

Mr. JONES arrives at the door, and "caves in" considerably.

3

DOMESTIC BLISS IN AUSTRALIA.

If you use Fitzumbug and Co.'s patent waterproof gossamer tent calico, you may defy Australian rain—as did the happy pair above depicted.

4

Topsy Turvey, – or, our Antipodes

1864–1869
From Criminal to Cosmopolitan

By the end of the 1860s the character of the colonies had changed from criminal to cosmopolitan with the arrival of thousands of immigrants who had come of their own free will. Moral standards, social behaviour, economic relations and class differences were continually adapting to the new character of the colonial society. Although there were many differences of opinion, one thing was agreed upon by all—with self-government, a strong economic foundation, and a new respectable population the time had come to shake off the shackles of the past and build a new nation to take its place in the world.

1 *Caution To Ladies* (Scott, *Sydney Punch*, 1865). Resourceful admirers find a way around even the formidable crinoline worn by 'Those pretty young ladies' who 'seated upon the skylight, wonder why all the gentlemen have left the deck, and what can be amusing them so much in the cabin'. But 'This is what amuses them so much' below the deck.

2 *Australia Has Other Sympathies Than Those With Crime—Dedicated, without permission to her Traducers* (Scott, *Sydney Punch*, 1864). Yet another plea to hasten the end of transportation—still operating to Western Australia—in order to lay the foundations of an optimistic and wealthy new nation, which would itself be able to provide Britain with funds and goods.

3 *Fashion And Famine* (Cousins, *Humbug*, 1869). The disparities in wealth that emerged after the gold rushes did much to exacerbate tensions in the colonies and underline the problems of the new immigrant.

1

CAUTION TO LADIES.

THOSE PRETTY YOUNG LADIES, SEATED UPON THE SKYLIGHT, WONDER WHY ALL THE GENTLEMEN HAVE LEFT THE DECK, AND WHAT AMUSING THEM SO MUCH IN THE CABIN.

This is what amuses them so much.

2

AUSTRALIA HAS OTHER SYMPATHIES THAN THOSE WITH CRIME.—*Dedicated, without permission, to her Traducers.*

3

FASHION AND FAMINE.

THE MAYOR'S BALL.
"With pleasure." £2 2*s*.

THE IMMIGRANTS' HOME.
"Can't afford it." 2*s*.

1865–1876
Fancy Fashions: What Next?

Although the fashions of the period came and went as they are wont to do, the crinoline was perhaps the dominant feature of contemporary dress. The original crinoline was made from horsehair and linen or cotton yarn. As a still-cotton fabric it was used as garment interlining, normally serving as a framework to fill out the large billowing skirts of the day. These provided excellent material for the cartoonist's pen. As in earlier and later periods, fashions seemed to go mad at times, leaving a nonplussed onlooker wondering exactly what would happen next.

1 *Possible Futurities* (Grieg, *Sydney Punch*, 1865). Even an upside-down crinoline was on the cards according to the wits of a generation bewildered by a rapid carousel of fashion fads.

2 *Fashion Gone Mad* (Scott, *Sydney Punch*, 1865). Each generation faces its challenge to the traditional sex differences in costume. In the 1860s women such as this who wore masculine clothing were branded 'Guys'.

3 *Similia Similibus Curantur* (*Sydney Punch*, 1865). If you can't beat them, join them. Crinolines were causing so much damage, in the popular legends of the day, that this cartoonist recommended a protective solution.

4 *Ye Geelonge Skating Rink and Matrimonial Recruiting Ground* (*Sam Slick in Victoria*, 1876). The ladies exhibit the bustle and the gents show off the correct attire of the day in a colonial version of that British 'pièce de résistance', the Sunday croquet game.

1

POSSIBLE FUTURITIES.

What *must* be the next eccentricity in female dress.

2

FASHION GONE MAD.

3

SIMILIA SIMILIBUS CURANTUR.

GUSHER having discoverd that the hooped-petticoats are impediments to locomotion, under circumstances like the above, has taken to wearing hoops in self-defence, and congratulates himself upon the result.

4

Ye Geelong Skating Rink and Matrimonial Recruiting Ground.

CHAPTER III

Wild Colonial Boys 1869–1900

Migrant Rubbish
King Bunny Forever
Horseless Coffins
The Sporting Life
Bring Out Your Dead
God and Mammon
Talking Wires
What Photography May Come To
Boneshakers
Birth Pangs
Fancy Fashions: What Next?

CHAPTER III
Wild Colonial Boys 1869–1900

The Little Boy from Manly

The Victorian age brought colonial cartooning to a peak. There were so many topics on which to comment that the profession attracted great artists whose imaginative work ushered in a golden age of black and white illustrating.

These artists could hardly have gone wrong, for they were witnesses to an exciting and unpredictable age in which a nation was being created before their very eyes. Intercolonial conferences, exhibitions and legislation served to bring the States together. The notion of a unified Australia became a reality with the creation of the Commonwealth and the construction of federal government machinery. The time had come for a national culture and an indigenous journal to express the birth of this newly found identity.

The first issue of the *Bulletin* appeared on January 31, 1880. Founded by John Haynes and John Archibald, it reached a circulation of 10 000 within five months, and eventually became the magazine that half of Australia wrote and all of Australia read. Brilliant artists such as Phil May and Livingstone Hopkins were imported at great expense for the new journal, and their style, more than any other, was handed on to the master of the succeeding generation—Norman Lindsay.

Even as a single nation was being created new divisions appeared like cracks from within. Working people began to organize unions that staged strikes on the waterfront and in the shearing sheds and the mines. Hard times unified workers and set them against the traditional rulers of the colonial world. Australian unions supported the Great Dock Strike of London in 1889 with a donation of £25 000, and two years later the first political Labor Party was formed in New South Wales with 36 members elected. The cartoonists also witnessed an early phase of feminism. Beginning in the late 1860s and gaining strength again in the 1890s, the women's movement rocked the conservative boat with its demands for equal rights.

Science and technology continued to advance at an ever-increasing rate. This was the generation that pioneered electricity; that greeted the first petrol engines and the prototype four-wheel motor car; these were the people who first heard of the flying machine and the Zeppelin airship, who first used the camera, saw moving film, and heard the phonograph and then the gramophone. Their world was changing every day.

The dynamism of the period infused the work of contemporary artists with gusto as they created a new, distinctly Australian brand of cartooning that was to become a model for the art in general. Several cartoonists trained in this school eventually left for Europe and the United States. Interestingly enough, the two mainstays of the period—Hopkins ('Hop') and May—were imports from the United States and Britain respectively, yet they fully responded to the emerging national identity. Entering the culture from abroad, they seemed to discern its distinctiveness more clearly. In their work they captured this new identity and fixed it for posterity. Their output is supplemented in this period by artists of the dying *Punch* school, as well as those from other, smaller journals which rose and fell with the fashions.

By now, the personification of the new colonies was more varied, for these were the people of the first free generation. The convict image was fading as the maidens asserted themselves and a new character appeared on the stage to represent the people—the Little Boy from Manly. A creation of Livingstone Hopkins, this figure was conceived after a lad at Manly caught the public eye by rushing forward to donate a penny to the Sudan War contingent in 1885. He became popular with other artists and represented the spirit of Australia until the Great War. The Australian people were throwing off the shackles of the past, determined to 'gallop over valleys and gallop over plains' for they 'scorned to live in slavery bound down by iron chains'. Nevertheless, although Australia was coming of age as it moved towards Federation, this was also the period of the 'bushman's bible' (the *Bulletin*), bushrangers, and 'Banjo' Paterson, when Australians liked to think of themselves as the *Wild Colonial Boys*.

Coming of age

1883–1897
Migrant Rubbish

Transportation may have been abolished in 1868 but this did not solve the problem of populating Australia with respectable citizens. The calibre of migrants worried the residents, particularly when it seemed that their jobs were at stake. The new arrivals were often referred to as 'rubbish' and became the target for many bigoted jokes. But with gold exhausted, the colonies lost much of their attraction to Europeans, who seemed to prefer the United States. Consequently, the colonies had to put up with, and make the most of, the people they could get—protests notwithstanding.

1 *Rubbish is not to be SHOT here!* (Hop, *Bulletin*, 1883). The locals resented the free immigrants, whom they saw as intruders of an inferior stock who had failed to make a success of their lives at home and had been forced to accept an assisted passage to the colonies.

2 *Landing Of "Forefathers" In Queensland* (Hop, *Bulletin*, 1895). With the creation of the 'Kanaka' slave trade in Queensland in 1862 another type of 'undesirable' came ashore. 'The South Sea Islanders now deport their criminals to Queensland where they are "absorbed" by the labor market.'

3 *Immigration!* (*Bulletin*, 1883). Although the gold rushes had attracted thousands to the colonies, the migrant stream was reduced to a trickle compared with the torrent that flowed to the United States during this period.

4 *Rubbish from the Cabbage-garden* (May, *Bulletin*, 1888). Victoria's Premier Gillies tips a barrel of 'Chow' rubbish onto the New South Wales garden of Premier Parkes.

5 *"Made In Germany": A Sketch on the arrival of the s.s. Friedrich der Grosse* (Eldridge, *Bulletin*, 1897). The country of origin mattered little; if they were foreigners then they were unpopular. With a depression undermining employment in the 1890s the locals feared migrants had come to take their jobs.

1

Rubbish is not to be SHOT here!

2

LANDING OF "FOREFATHERS" IN QUEENSLAND.
The South Sea Islanders now deport their criminals to Queensland where they are "absorbed" by the Labor market.

3

IMMIGRATION!

4

Rubbish from the Cabbage-garden.
Premier Gillies sends the Chow Invasion on to Premier Parkes.

5

"MADE IN GERMANY": A sketch on the arrival of the s.s. Friedrich der Grosse.

1884–1893
King Bunny Forever

By the 1880s the rabbit had become the number one pest to the colonial farmer. Released accidentally in 1859, the rabbit spread and thrived on Australian grasses and climate and multiplied in the hundreds of thousands. At times it appeared that hills were moving as there were so many rabbits roving over them. It was nothing for hundreds to be shot in a day, and in 1868 the visiting Prince Alfred and three untrained companions bagged 203. As they eat many grasses, vegetables, young trees, grape vines and crops, rabbits were a great nuisance to farmers and also threatened the existence of many native plants and animals. Protective fences were of little use and it was not until myxomatosis was introduced by the CSIRO in 1950 that King Bunny was dethroned forever.

1 *A Modern St. Patrick* (Hop, *Bulletin*, 1885). All methods were tried in an attempt to get rid of the rabbit. There were even suggestions from the Church that the squatters resort to prayers.

2 *"The King Is Dead; Long Live The King"* (Cantle, *Australasian Pastoralists Review*, 1893). Graziers feared that unless it was checked, the rabbit would ruin their precious wool industry.

3 *The Rabbit Question* (Hop, *Bulletin*, 1888). In the folk mythology of the outback, rabbits grew to an enormous size.

4 *In Tophet—The Man-Pest At Rabbitville* (*Bulletin*, 1888). The tables are turned in the imagination of one cartoonist, who takes the rabbit plague to its logical extreme.

5 *It's The Climate* (*Melbourne Punch*, 1884). Many 'tall stories' proliferated as rabbits spread in waves over the continent.

1

A Modern St. Patrick.

2

"THE KING IS DEAD; LONG LIVE THE KING."

3

The Rabbit Question.

4

IN TOPHET.—THE MAN-PEST AT RABBITVILLE.

5

IT'S THE CLIMATE.

ALARMING DEVELOPMENT OF THE RABBIT IN AUSTRALIA.

1882–1888
Horseless Coffins

Following the successful use of locomotives in hauling coal wagons at collieries in England in 1812, Stephenson adapted James Watt's steam engine to provide the first passenger rail service from Stockton to Darlington in 1825. The steam train was so successful that by 1840 there were 2 140 kilometres of railway track in Britain. In the colonies the first line opened in 1854 when a private company provided a steam railway between Flinders Street (Melbourne) and Port Melbourne. The following year steam trains began running between Sydney and Parramatta. Rail services were soon springing up to provide faster and smoother transport for those who were travelling in the antipodes. These journeys were not always without incident.

1 *A Shake Of The Hand* (*Sydney Punch*, 1882). Although the two major colonies were linked by rail by 1883, the gauge of the respective tracks was different and so necessitated a change of trains at Albury on the border.

2 *How We Make Our Railways* (*Bulletin*, 1883). The construction of railways which began in the eastern colonies in the 1850s became the subject for many jokes. Here 'you have the line as originally surveyed, and a proposed deviation. Which is which? Well you "pays your money and you takes your choice"—especially you "pays your money".'

3 *Coffin Engines* (*Melbourne Punch*, 1884). Accidents were becoming so frequent by the 1880s that trains were dubbed 'horseless coffins'. Among the problems of rail travel were faulty brakes, rickety bridges that collapsed and lines that subsided into the quagmire produced by rain.

4 *Non-Colliding System Of Railways* (*Melbourne Punch*, 1884). The wits of the day devised their own solutions for trains that had a tendency to collide head on.

5 *Railroad Speed* (*Melbourne Punch*, 1888). Jokes about slow trains were particularly apt in the colonies where distances were so great and journeys so long.

1

A SHAKE OF THE HAND!

2

HOW WE MAKE OUR RAILWAYS.

3

COFFIN ENGINES.

The latest novelty on the Victorian Railways.

4

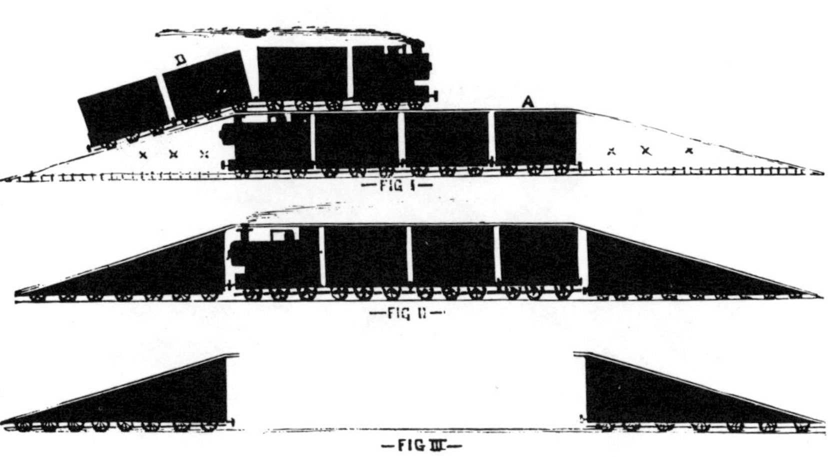

NON-COLLIDING SYSTEM OF RAILWAYS.

5

RAILROAD SPEED.

Sale; distance from Melbourne 127 miles. Time taken, 6¼ hours.

THE START. THE ARRIVAL.

1869–1893
The Sporting Life

Sport did not take long to gain a hold of the emerging nation. Cricket, inherited from the old country, became popular when the first English Eleven toured the colonies in the 1850s. Football evolved in the different colonies in a variety of codes, with the local Australian Rules becoming established in the southern colonies by the turn of the century. Horse-racing also became extremely popular, and such events as the Melbourne Cup were being run by 1861. As always, sport had its detractors, but, as usual, it won the day.

1 *In the Toils* (*Bulletin*, 1885). It was felt that money would ruin the 'Sport of Kings' when admission fees were introduced and 'professional' players, who kept a sharper eye on the gate-money than the ball, were enlisted. Many thought that this would result in the death of amateur cricket.

2 *Kicked Out!* (*Bulletin*, 1883). In the early days, the roughness of the colonial style of football aroused considerable opposition to its adoption.

3 *The Cricketress* (Minns, *Bulletin*, 1885). Sportswomen did not escape the cartoonist's pen when they walked onto the pitch.

4 *Patrons of the Turf* (Cousins, *Humbug*, 1869). The character of the patrons of the turf gave some cause for concern during the early years of the Melbourne Cup, with bribery influencing the performance of some horses and poison limiting the chances of others.

5 *The Cup That Jeers* (*Melbourne Punch*, 1893). There was considerable opposition to the annual running of the Melbourne Cup in the early days with anti-Semitic jibes being the order of the day.

1

2

Kicked Out!

3

4

5

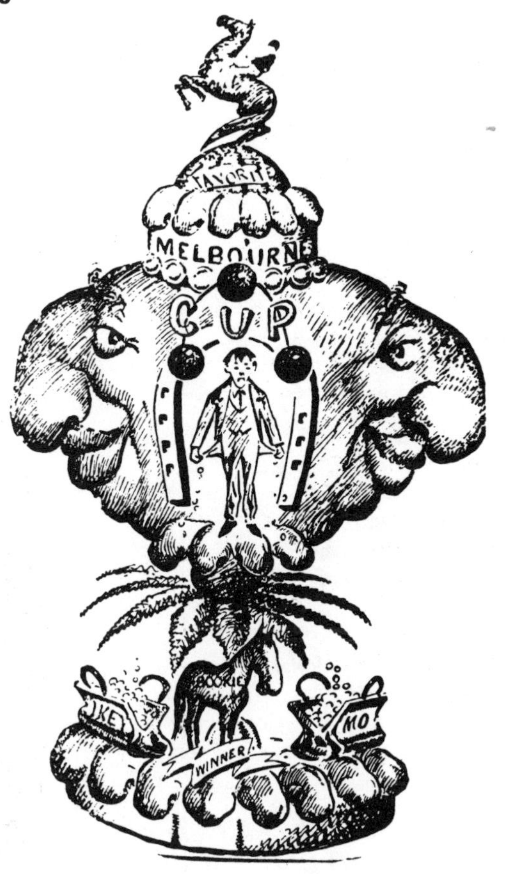

THE CUP THAT JEERS.

DESIGN FOR THE MELBOURNE CUP.

(And we may add that it is sure to be won by a nose.

1869–1888
Bring Out Your Dead

During this period recurring cholera and smallpox epidemics swept through Victoria and New South Wales, claiming many lives. As many as 30 out of every 100 people died in some of the areas worst hit by smallpox. The poor state of public health caused by lack of sanitation, primitive sewerage and contaminated water placed most settlements in a dangerous position. Because cholera and smallpox are highly contagious diseases and tend to spread quickly, local residents lived in fear until the discovery of prophylactic vaccination.

1 *Bring Out Your Dead; or, What it may come to* (Carrington, *Melbourne Punch*, 1869). The increasing death toll from smallpox and cholera epidemics reminded people of the Black Plague, which had decimated England in the seventeenth century.

2 *A Ghost That Ought To Be laid* (Carrington, *Melbourne Punch*, 1870). The streets of Melbourne reek with the stench of disease as the cholera and typhus miasma rises like a spirit from the bodies of hundreds who died in the relentless epidemic of the 1870s.

3 *By Appointment, Successor To The Kiama Ghost* (*Bulletin*, 1888). The representation of smallpox as a Chinaman reveals the popular fear that it was the Chinese who were introducing the dreaded disease.

4 *Punch's Contribution To The Nightingale Testimonial* (Chevalier, *Melbourne Punch*, 1869). The practice of hospital hygiene had been pioneered by Florence Nightingale during the Crimean War. With cleaner homes and hospitals the incidence of contagious diseases decreased markedly in the colonies.

1

"BRING OUT YOUR DEAD;"
OR,
WHAT IT MAY COME TO.

2

A GHOST THAT OUGHT TO BE LAID.

[See preceding page.

3

BY APPOINTMENT, SUCCESSOR TO THE KIAMA GHOST.

4

THE PAST;

MRS. GAMP, CASHIERED.

THE FUTURE

FLORENCE NIGHTINGALE, PROMOTED,

1875–1900
God and Mammon

The divisions within the Church amused cartoonists during the period as the various denominations fought with the State over the right to control education. The battle for government financial aid raged through the 1870s in most colonies although in 1872 the Victorian government established a lead with a 'free, compulsory and secular' education system. The Church had fallen into disrespect through land deals in Victoria, while in other areas the men of God were accused of materialism, corruption, hypocrisy and a general abuse of Christianity.

1 *Sad Result Of Free Education* (*Bulletin*, 1885). Free education was introduced in Victoria in 1872 and in New South Wales in 1880. The other colonies followed in due course despite the opposition to the new policy of enlightenment.

2 *The Fishwives—Or The Quarrel At The Cross-Roads* (Hop, *Bulletin*, 1900). Like a pair of stubborn old fishwives the Catholic and Protestant Churches fight for control over the minds and souls of the emerging Australian nation.

3 *Colonial Fetishism; Or, Modern Idolatry* (McLeod, *Sydney Punch*, 1875). Governments, churches, professors and people from all ranks of society offer their prayers and gifts to Mammon in a society whose religion is materialism and whose god is money.

1

SAD RESULT OF FREE EDUCATION.

2

THE FISHWIVES—OR THE QUARREL AT THE CROSS-ROADS.

COLONIAL FETICHISM; OR, MODERN IDOLATRY.

HURRAH for the God of Gold!
Shout for the great King Mammon!
Whose works in the days of old
Bear fruit in the days of gammon.

For who among us hath respect
If gifted not with wealth?
And poverty is the worst of crimes,
And few do good by stealth.

Then— Hurrah for the God of Gold!
Shout for the great King Mammon;
Whose works in the days of old
Are renewed in the days of gammon.

1865–1888
Talking Wires

The inventions of the age caused great excitement in the colonies. Although London had been lit by gaslight since 1812, this new form of illumination did not reach the colonial towns until the late 1850s and early 1860s. If that was an improvement on oil and candlepower then the telegraph, which reached South Australia from Darwin in 1872, was truly a modern miracle. However, the introduction of the telephone in 1878 represented the ultimate in 'talking wires'.

1 *Gas In Melbourne* (*Melbourne Punch*, 1865). The introduction of gas lighting caused quite a stir in Melbourne and many brought up on candles and oil lamps could not at first understand the new miracle.

2 *The Battle Of The Gas Companies* (*Melbourne Punch*, 1886). Private companies fought long and hard for the contract to light the streets of Melbourne and Sydney, which by this time had a combined population approaching one million.

3 *Danger Ahead* (*Melbourne Punch*, 1884). Sydney, Melbourne and Adelaide were connected by telegraph in 1858 and Tasmania was brought into the network by submarine cable the following year. Perth was finally linked to the eastern cities in 1877.

4 *Why She Wanted The Wire* (Hop, *Bulletin*, 1888). The 'bustle' of the day is imitated by Aborigines taking advantage of the overland telegraph from Darwin to Adelaide, which was completed in 1872 to put the colonies in direct contact with England for the first time.

5 *The Height Of Imagination* (*Melbourne Punch*, 1885). The introduction of the telephone in 1878 and the creation of the first public exchange in Melbourne in 1880 inspired a fresh spate of jokes about the confusing new-fangled invention.

6 *Sermons In Telephones* (*Melbourne Punch*, 1886). The new invention brings the word of God to the people in an imaginary application of the receiver.

1

GAS IN MELBOURNE.

FIRST SON OF THE SOIL: That's a precious rum kind of a lamp that is, my word!

SECOND SON OF THE SOIL: My oath, it is *so*! Where the —— —— do they put the *hile*.

2

THE BATTLE OF THE GAS COMPANIES.

FIRST COMPANY.—*I'll sell at seven and six.*

SECOND DO.—*I'll give it away!*

FIRST DO.—*I'll give the public ten shillings a thousand to take it!*

SECOND DO.—*I'll punch your lantern!*

FIRST DO.—*Do it! Ugh!*

SECOND DO.—*Come on! Ugh!*

MR. PUNCH.—*Go it, Gentlemen! while you're ruining yourselves we get cheap gas.*

DANGER AHEAD.

"Confound those telegraph wires though!"

4

WHY SHE WANTED THE WIRE.

5

THE HEIGHT OF IMAGINATION.

Teetotaller (through the telephone).—"I WISH YOU'D STAND A LITTLE FURTHER AWAY; YOUR BREATH SMELLS OF WHISKY."

6

SERMONS IN TELEPHONES.

1. Mary Anne can cook the dinner and attend to the service. 2. A shave and a sermon. 3. Anybody can be good now. 4. "Now then, Maria, hurry up, the church bells are ringing." 5. Even in time we may be able to reach the poor lubra in the wild bush with a sermon by the bishop himself.

1885–1888 What Photography May Come To

Although the Daguerreotype photograph was created in 1839, the art did not become popular until George Eastman introduced the Kodak box camera in 1888. With this simple snapshot camera, which could be used by amateurs, photography soon became a universal hobby. The early Kodak camera contained a roll of film with 100 exposures. The photographer returned the camera containing the film to the Eastman company, which then developed the film, printed the pictures, and returned the camera with a new film. With the invention of celluloid in 1889, the future of photography and film was assured.

1 *New And Ingenious Ready-Acting Dog-Tail And Camera Attachment, For Tourists* (*Bulletin*, 1885). A satirical advertisement heralding the arrival of yet another modern miracle.

2 *Dad: 'Ere, 'old this tram-ticket; it'll show you was took in Sydney* (Cross, *Smith's Weekly*, 1938). A later cartoon shows how long the colonials took to get used to the new inventions as Dad and Dave go on camera for the first time.

3 *The New Burglar Trap* (*Melbourne Punch*, 1888). The camera was imaginatively applied to a burglar alarm, which also harnessed the recently arrived electric light and a phonograph that shouts 'Police' into a telephone connected to the local station.

4 *The Pacific Mail Steamers from Sydney to San Francisco are to be taken off* (*Bulletin*, 1885). Suggestions for linking Sydney with America included a trans-Pacific railway, a mail-carrying balloon, swimming postmen and carrier pigeons.

5 *What Photography may come to* (Grieg, *Sydney Punch*, 1888). Photography became so popular that everybody wanted to be in on the act. Here ragamuffins make fun of the boom in street photography.

1

NEW AND INGENIOUS READY-ACTING DOG-TAIL AND CAMERA ATTACHMENT, FOR TOURISTS.

A patent is now pending by the inventors.

They claim the dog's tail and the instantaneous shutter, also the combination of the shutter and dog's tail, also the whole dog, and the general application, in the manner substantially and for the purpose described.

2

Dad: 'Ere, 'old this tram-ticket; it'll show you was took in Sydney.

3

THE NEW BURGLAR TRAP.

4

5

What Photography may come to.

STREET BOY—"Now then Hartis, for a ha'porth of beauty."

1885–1897
Boneshakers

Bicycles were being made commercially in London by 1866 but did not reach the colonies until the 1880s. At first the penny-farthing, developed in 1870, was the most popular bicycle, but the difficulty of climbing onto a seat perched above the 131-centimetre diameter front-drive wheel encouraged the invention of the safety bicycle in 1885 with chain drive and wheels of equal size. John Dunlop fitted the first pneumatic tyres in 1888, free wheels were adopted in 1894 and variable gears were applied in 1899. By the 1890s cycling had become a craze throughout the colonies.

1 *Our New Australian Coat Of Arms* (*Melbourne Punch*, 1896). Australian bicyclists did so well in early international races that a new coat of arms was suggested.

2 *Getting Into Condition* (Eldridge, *Bulletin*, 1897). Nobody was too fat to mount the new 'safety bicycle' which, unlike the penny-farthing, had two smaller wheels of equal size.

3 *The Aerocycle* (*Melbourne Punch*, 1896). A technological speculation inspired by the rapid development of the bicycle.

4 *What To Wear On A Wheel* (Vincent, *Melbourne Punch*, 1896). Conservative members of society recommended the establishment of a committee comprising doctors, dressmakers and 'a captain of society' to 'consider and evolve an appropriate costume for the cyclist'. Mr Punch had his own suggestions.

5 *Hem! Behold A Dashing Young Wheelman Of Today* (*Bulletin*, 1885). What every well-dressed young beau was wearing on the penny-farthing.

6 *The Advent Of The Bike—"One Of The Unemployed"* (Levy, *Bulletin*, 1897). The new form of transport became so popular that many believed the day of the horse to be over.

1

OUR NEW AUSTRALIAN COAT OF ARMS.

2

GETTING INTO CONDITION.

3

The Aerocycle

4

WHAT TO WEAR ON A WHEEL.

5

6

THE ADVENT OF THE BIKE—"ONE OF THE UNEMPLOYED.

1887–1900
Birth Pangs

The Diamond Jubilee of Queen Victoria was celebrated no less in the colonies than elsewhere in the Empire, especially as Royal assent was being sought for the creation of the bold new Commonwealth. Leading Australian dignitaries travelled to London for the royal celebrations, and festivities were organized in every State. The decade before Federation was marked by a rising tide of national consciousness despite, or perhaps even because of, the economic depression, which began in 1890 and lasted for many years. The drought, the bank crash and the failed strikes dampened but did not defeat a people determined to win nationhood and to forge a future for themselves.

1 *A Jubilee Medal* (*Bulletin*, 1887). Preoccupied with the threat of yellow hordes, some Australians saw the jubilee of Queen Victoria as an appropriate time to repatriate the Chinese. Following an intercolonial conference in 1888, legislation restricting Chinese immigration was passed in New South Wales.

2 *Rival Subscription Lists* (May, *Bulletin*, 1897). A disaster in the mining industry, which left many widows without means of income, inspired some to recommend that money spent on the jubilee would be better spent on the widows and children of the dead coal-miners.

3 *The Latest Addition To The Family* (Hop, *Bulletin*, 1899). Although most of the States had agreed to federate by the turn of the century, Queensland wavered because of its dependence on the black-slave trade that the other States demanded it terminate as a condition of membership in the new nation. Western Australia, uncertain to the last, joined in after a referendum. Here, Edmund Barton holds the new arrival.

4 *How's That?* (*Melbourne Punch*, 1897). Women who had been pressing for equal rights for years began to make headway as the century turned.

1

A JUBILEE MEDAL.

2

Rival Subscription-Lists.

5 *Laying The Corner-Stone Of The Australian Commonwealth* (Hop, *Bulletin*, 1900). The first Prime Minister, Edmund Barton, drinks from the bottle, the Churches compete in federation prayers and poets and musicians outdo each other in the national celebration.

3

4

HOW'S THAT?

5

LAYING THE CORNER-STONE OF THE AUSTRALIAN COMMONWEALTH. By Hop's Understudy.

1879–1897
Fancy Fashions: What Next?

Any period that experienced such scientific and technological changes was bound to witness unusual experiments in clothing. Although the fashion carousel brought a considerable variety with each revolution, the garment that stuck longest was perhaps the bustle. A pad or a frame which accentuated the hips and posterior, the bustle caused nothing less than a sensation. Women's clothes were also adapting to the Australian climate as well as reflecting the increased social and political freedom that women had recently gained. Nevertheless the ladies who now rode bicycles, smoked cigars and swam in the sea left the gentlemen of the period wondering just what would happen next.

1 *"He-Haws" And "Cacklers"* (*Melbourne Punch*, 1884). The more fashionable members of society were always the butt of cartoonists' jokes.

2 *At The "At Home"* (Souter, *Bulletin*, 1897). A daring midriff is exposed ahead of its time.

3 *Our Suburban Mode* (*Sydney Punch*, 1880). Fashionable ladies who were seen parading—in this case with outlandish hairstyles and long gloves—often scandalized social gatherings.

4 *What Next?* (*Bulletin*, 1896). The advent of the bicycle had liberated women to the extent that anything now seemed possible. The adoption of pantaloons allowed females to ride bicycles in comfort and safety.

5 *Amelia—How Do You Like Your First Cigar?* (*Sam Slick in Victoria*, 1879). Women caused a sensation in 'high society' when they began smoking. Although at first they only smoked in private, it was not long before they took up smoking in public.

1

"HE-HAWS" AND "CACKLERS."
INTERIOR OF A BOX ANY FASHIONABLE NIGHT AT ONE OF OUR THEATRES.

2

AT THE "AT HOME."
SHE: "*What nonsense—not hear my song, indeed! Why, everything was perfectly quiet.*"
HE: "*My dear, you forget your costume.*"

3

OUR SUBURBAN MODE.

4

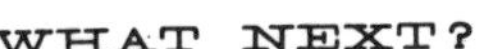

WHAT NEXT?

5

AMELIA.— HOW DO YOU LIKE YOUR FIRST CIGAR
BELDA (PUFFING) ITS GRAND I FEEL LIKE SIR WALTER RALEIGH
AMELIA DO YOU REALLY THAT MUST BE A SENSATION

CHAPTER IV

One People: One Prejudice 1901–1913

Horsetralia for the Asstralians
Enter New Woman
Death of the Sundowners
Plagues and Pollution
Police 'Protection'
Electrical Marvels
The Motor Car
Learning to Fly
Taking to the Water
Fancy Fashions: What Next?

CHAPTER IV
One People: One Prejudice 1901–1913

Mulga Bill of the future—a Yellow Fancy

The domestic divisions that had emerged in the years preceding the federation of the Australian States continued to inspire cartoonists working after 1901. However, international crises were looming, and to many it seemed that the period was little more than a build-up to a major war. Meanwhile, the young nation had more than enough to concern itself with at home, and cartoonists were never lacking in material.

The States had been drawn together under federation and the subsequent lifting of internal trade barriers. The population was still relatively small and did not reach four million until 1905. There was an acute sense of insecurity in the air. The Japanese posed the main external threat following their victory over the Russians in 1905. Thus it was not surprising, given the uncertainty of the world situation, that the first Act of the new Commonwealth government should be the Immigration Restriction Act (1901), which established the basis of the 'White Australia' policy.

Permission was gained from Britain to establish a Royal Australian Navy, and the first warships were acquired in 1910. The following year a locally built destroyer, the *Warrego*, was launched and compulsory military service for young men between the ages of twelve and twenty-six was introduced. Sydney and Melbourne were linked by telephone in 1907, and in 1912 work on the trans-Australian railway was begun. The first Commonwealth census was taken in 1911 and the Commonwealth Bank started operations in 1912. In 1913, a site having finally been agreed upon, Australia's capital was named Canberra and the foundation stone was laid.

Political and social movements directed towards equality for women gained pace, prompted by the general push towards democratic liberties and individual rights. Women had sought equality since the 1860s but it was only around the turn of the century that their impact really began to be felt. They had won the vote in all States by 1908, and many took advantage of their greater social freedom. The old class structure was given a shake-down when the Labor Party was elected to govern in 1904 and again in 1910. The twentieth century was heralded down under by a progressive note.

The rulers of the previous century were dying out, replaced or deposed by the leaders of the new. In Britain, Edward VII came to the throne upon the death of Victoria in 1901. In other countries, the transition between rulers was not so peaceful. Leaders were assassinated in the United States and Russia, revolutions created new regimes in Portugal, Mexico and China and threats of war were issued by Italian and German leaders bent on restructuring the European map that had not changed since the days of Napoleon.

When they did come—those shots at Sarajevo that triggered the Great War of 1914—they gave the Australian nation something it had been searching for, something it lacked. As yet without a flag or a national anthem, and in internal disagreement about the site of the national capital, the newly created country was waiting to be tested.

Cartoonists were also interested in the social problems of the time, such as ill-health and pollution, that worried the emerging Commonwealth. The good old days of bush hospitality had, with the death of the 'sundowners', given way to the urban realities of large impersonal cities. Cartoonists mapped the light-hearted events of the day, but also saw themselves as fierce critics of corruption and graft. Thus it is not surprising to find many attacks on institutions such as the Victorian police force, which came under heavy fire.

Punch bids farewell during this time as cartoonists of the *Bulletin* achieve supremacy in the art. 'Hop' continued to delight the journal's readers, but by the close of the period Norman Lindsay had established himself as the master. The Little Boy from Manly continued to represent Australia until he was replaced, in 1914, by an older, less naive figure. However, the maidens lingered on to represent the States. Despite the disagreements and differences, there was one thing on which all Australians were united, and that was their fear of racial contamination. Exaggerated by the chauvinism that belongs to a young country arriving late on the stage of history, the mood of the period is perhaps best summed up as *One People: One Prejudice.*

The Little Boy from Manly makes way for a new national identity

1902–1909 Horsetralia for the Asstralians

The new nation was faced with a dilemma that had worried the various colonies from the start: migrants were desperately needed but the country would suffer if too many 'undesirables' were allowed in. By the turn of the century the population was still only 3 750 000, too small either to defend the shores in the event of attack or to provide the workforce needed to develop the young Commonwealth. The Chinese and Kanakas had previously supplemented the workforce but the Immigration Restriction and Pacific Island Labourers' Acts of 1901 created a 'White Australia' policy barring their entry. Australia now had to advertise in earnest for the Anglo-Saxon migrants it so badly needed.

1 *Horsetralia for the Asstralians* (Hop, *Bulletin*, 1902). The Imperial lion and the Australian sheep unite to defend the new nation from all but white British migrants.

2 *To Gain Cohen's Blessing* (Lindsay, *Bulletin*, 1902). The Immigration Restriction and Pacific Island Labourer's Acts were criticized by John Bull who had recently saved businesses in South Africa by using coloured labour. Here he tries to persuade the first Prime Minister, Edmund Barton, to accept the Kanakas and Chinese, who had helped develop the country to date.

3 *"Advertising Australia"* (Zif, *Australian Worker*, 1909). Many felt that Australia's overseas advertisements for migrants were misleading. As this satirical brochure indicates, the myth of the good life could grow out of all proportion to the reality that awaited the new Australians.

1

2

TO GAIN COHEN'S BLESSING.

3

"ADVERTISING AUSTRALIA."

1884–1900
Enter New Woman

Taking their lead from the Women's Suffrage Associations in Britain and the United States, local groups obtained the vote for women in South Australia in 1894, Western Australia in 1899, New South Wales in 1902, Tasmania in 1903, Queensland in 1905 and Victoria in 1908. By 1902 women were voting in the federal elections and exerting an influence far greater than their counterparts in Europe. The first feminist wave had been successful.

1 *A New Terror For Australia* (Hop, *Bulletin*, 1892). According to the London *Evening Standard*, 'There are thousands of young men wanting wives in Australia where there are few wives to be had. There is a colonial career open to our surplus female population if they can get to the other side of the globe!'

2 *A Domestic Matter* (Hop, *Bulletin*, 1898). Women in all walks of life took heart from the 'New Woman' movement, which challenged many social traditions including employer/servant relations.

3 *On the Word of a Woman—An Everyday Occurrence* (Lindsay, *Bulletin*, 1900). Lindsay portrays the *femme fatale*—with the devil over her shoulder and the skull above—as the wicked cause of a man being jailed for rape.

4 *The New Woman's New Year* (*Melbourne Punch*, 1896). The 'New Woman' overtakes the ageing leader to establish a vigorous example.

5 *Athletics For Ladies* (*Melbourne Punch*, 1884). With recently gained strength the 'better half' informs her 'hubby', 'Oh dear no; he's not going out to dinner by his little selfy selfy, he's going to take his poor little wifey to the theatre tonight, and to the Derby on Saturday, that's what he's going to do'.

6 *Going Out! The Passing of the New Woman* (*Melbourne Punch*, 1893). The first feminist flame flickers before going out. The new women's movement was regarded as a passing aberration.

1

A NEW TERROR FOR AUSTRALIA.

2

A DOMESTIC MATTER.

3

4

THE NEW WOMAN'S NEW YEAR.

5

ATHLETICS FOR LADIES.

6

GOING OUT!

1893–1905 Death of the Sundowners

Many people who lost their jobs during the economic depression of the 1890s took to the bush. For years they were offered piecemeal work and tucker in lieu of wages. The more cunning among them would arrive at the homestead just as the sun went down so that it was too late for them to do any work that day. Then, having enjoyed the evening meal traditionally offered to them on the understanding that they would do odd jobs in the morning, they slipped away at first light. The 'sundowners' got away with it in good years but when drought struck, the homestead gates were finally closed to them.

1 *An Impression Of The Melbourne Pageant—The Unemployed Arch* (Hop, *Bulletin*, 1901). Even as the first federal parliament was being opened by the Duke of York and Cornwall, unemployment was becoming a major issue.

2 *A Merry Devil* (*Bulletin*, 1905). Even in Hell the sundowner is unable to find work.

3 *As In A Glass Darkly* (Lindsay, *Bulletin*, 1905). Many of the sundowners 'knocked back their cheque' as soon as they were paid.

4 *A Drought-Resisting Stock* (Hop, *Bulletin*, 1903). In the drought years early in the century water was so scarce that boiling the billy was often an impossibility.

5 *The Death Of Australian Hospitality* (Hop, *Bulletin*, 1893). The new policy towards sundowners became official when the Associated Pastoralists announced that they would no longer supply swagmen with free rations. Starvation clings to the back of the traveller.

1

AN IMPRESSION OF THE MELBOURNE PAGEANT.—THE UNEMPLOYED ARCH.

2

A MERRY DEVIL.

SUNDOWNER *(just arrived)*: *"Got any work, boss?"*

THE BOSS: *"Work! We don't work here! There's been smoke-oh ever since I remember."*

3

AS IN A GLASS DARKLY.

DRUNK: "*Lemme get at him! I tell yer that's the bloke wot made me do in me sixty quid.*"

4

A DROUGHT-RESISTING STOCK.
THE AUSTRALIAN OF THE FUTURE, WHO WILL ONLY CARRY A BILLY THROUGH FORCE OF HABIT.

5

THE DEATH OF AUSTRALIAN HOSPITALITY.

1900–1911
Plagues and Pollution

Pollution in various forms was often a by-product of the latest inventions. Steam trains covered curious passengers with soot when they were game enough to look out of the window or whenever the train passed through a tunnel. Steamers deposited a layer of black grit on those adventurous enough to stand on deck, and horse-drawn vehicles left a trail of manure that nourished flies and annoyed pedestrians. The sewage and much of the city garbage was often cast out to sea whence it sometimes found its way back to the beaches. Coupled with a general lack of hygiene it is no wonder that outbreaks of plague and smallpox occurred from time to time.

1 *In The Grip Of Contagion* (Marquet, *Table Talk*, 1904). The smallpox epidemic that gripped Tasmania in 1904 induced government officials to improve sanitary arrangements.

2 *Rat-Tat-Tat* (Hop, *Bulletin*, 1900). Rats overran Sydney during the 1890s, causing a spate of diseases, including a form of the plague. Shortly after the turn of the century this spread to Melbourne.

3 *When The Garbage Comes Home* (Lindsay, *Bulletin*, 1911). An early pollution cartoon showing the rubbish dumped on Sydney beaches was subtitled, 'The Sea Hath its Pearls—and other things'.

4 *Politeness* (Lindsay, *Bulletin*, 1905). Smoking in public was forbidden for 'respectable' women around the turn of the century. Cigarettes did not supplant pipes and cigars until after the Great War.

5 *Some Melbourne Matters* (Durkin, *Bulletin*, 1900). Although horse droppings were a major problem before the advent of the car, the local government was loath to spend money cleaning up the mess, especially in Melbourne where in 1900 the Lord Mayor voted against awarding dung carters the minimum wage.

1

IN THE GRIP OF CONTAGION.

2

RAT-TAT-TAT!

3

WHEN THE GARBAGE COMES HOME.

4

POLITENESS.

LUBRA : *"Say, boss, you objec' ladies smokin'?"*

5

SOME MELBOURNE MATTERS.

1896–1914
Police 'Protection'

Allegations concerning corruption and brutality in the colonial police force began soon after the initial 'Loyal Associations' were formed in the early 1800s. Former convicts had been recruited in the early days, especially in Sydney where John Redmond and George Barrington reached the ranks of Chief Constable and Superintendent respectively. Fear of the police was strong in Melbourne in the depression of the 1890s, when many turned to crime in order to stay alive, but police behaviour was such that by the outbreak of the Great War journalists were demanding protection from the police and inquiries into their practices.

1 *A Matter Of Competition* (Low, *Bulletin*, 1914). There were few police and they were either inefficient or turned a blind eye to crime during the early years of the twentieth century. Here Sydney burglars have a heyday.

2 *Standing-Room Only* (Vincent, *Bulletin*, 1896). The inadequacy of public hospitals was revealed when an epidemic struck Melbourne in 1896.

3 *The Third Degree* (*Melbourne Punch*, 1913). Brutality was a major issue for the critics of the Victorian force, who claimed that police used violence when interviewing suspects.

4 *Moving Pictures* (*Bulletin*, 1912). 'The Great Train Robbery' (1905), one of the first films made, was so popular that a spate of 'cops and robbers' films followed.

5 *Procession To-day. Beware of the Police* (*Melbourne Punch*, 1913). People demonstrating on political, economic or military issues received such rough handling from the Victorian police that the press ran a campaign to gain public protection from the force.

1

A MATTER OF COMPETITION.

2

STANDING-ROOM ONLY.

The Condition of the Melbourne Hospitals in the Hour of Need.

3

The man who looks as if he knows something is taken in and plied with questions for 24 hours.—Note the pliers.

4

Moving pictures are held to be a contributing cause of the recent crime wave.

5

1911–1914
Electrical Marvels

Electricity arrived just in time to brighten up Australia on the eve of the Commonwealth celebrations. In 1900 the lights of the Sydney Town Hall were turned on, giving many their first glimpse of the new illumination. The message 'One People: One Destiny' leapt out across the night sky to herald a new century and new nation. In Melbourne, the Exhibition building was decorated with 10 000 light bulbs for the opening of Federal Parliament in 1901. According to one journal, 'Melbourne was scribbled over with electric fires in the most gigantic scheme of pyrotechnics ever attempted in the Southern Hemisphere'.

1 *Overstocked* (Minns, *Bulletin*, 1914). The gramophone, which was invented in 1887 by Emil Berliner, became very popular around the turn of the century in Australia.

2 *Outside The Hotel Lift* (McCrae, *Melbourne Punch*, 1911). Although mechanical lifts had been carrying goods since the late eighteenth century it was not until 1857 that the elevator was introduced. This invention, along with the manufacture of steel, opened the way for the skyscraper.

3 *The Electric Home* (Nuttall, *Melbourne Punch*, 1913). Although many homes were wired before the turn of the century electricity was by no means common and the new form of power remained a novelty up to the Great War.

1

OVERSTOCKED.

DEALER: "*You buy that feller, Jacky?*"
JACKY: "*No feah! One plurry talkin' machine's 'nuff for me.*"

2

OUTSIDE THE HOTEL LIFT.

"'E let me ride in that thing up to the ceilin' an' down again three times for half a sov. It was so blamed cheap 'e wouldn't let me pay in front of the others!"

A "SHOCKING" HOME.

1905–1914
The Motor Car

The construction of the petrol engine by Daimler in 1882 opened the way for the motor car. In 1885, Benz demonstrated a prototype running on one cylinder but Diesel developed the forerunner of the modern car with his refined petrol engine of 1892. This was placed on four wheels for a successful demonstration by Benz in 1893, and it was then only a matter of time before the new mode of transport became commercially viable. Australians first saw the car when it was imported to Sydney in 1897. Soon there were privately owned cars on the roads and by 1905 motor buses and motor cabs were in operation in Melbourne and Sydney. The first T-model Ford rolled off the assembly line in 1908.

1 *Motor Punishment In Sheol* (Brown, *Bulletin*, 1905). Goggles were essential for the driver of the motorcar before the days of closed cabins and windscreens. Sheol, of course, is Hell.

2 *The Breaker* (Lindsay, *Bulletin*, 1914). The characteristics of the new horseless carriage were not always immediately understood, especially in the bush.

3 *The Ruling Passion* (Lindsay, *Bulletin*, 1905). Until the cars got faster early motor accidents were something of a joke, a mere diversion from the usual preoccupations of the day.

4 *At The Show* (*Melbourne Punch*, 1911). To the amusement of the old-fashioned, early motorists spent as much time under the bonnet as at the wheel.

5 *Still In Action* (*Melbourne Punch*, 1910). The Prime Minister, Alfred Deakin, during a New South Wales tour had, in one week, four motor, two railway and two buggy accidents. Here he is grateful that he did not try an aeroplane.

1

MOTOR PUNISHMENT IN SHEOL.

DIABOLUS: *"How yon eyeballs glare."*

REPLYUS: *"So would yours if you had to turn the corners through all eternity."*

2

THE BREAKER.

PASSENGER: *"Look out, Bronco! Here comes a motor-car."*

BRONCO: *"Well, they can't blame me if I bust 'em up. Stinker's bolted."*

3

THE RULING PASSION.
JOHNNY *(as the car bumps him)*: *" B' Jove, I believe she smiled."*

4

FARMER HAYKOKK (as chauffeur dives under motor).—" And yet they say the city blokes ain't shy."

5

STILL IN ACTION.

1913–1914
Learning to Fly

Although balloons had been successfully flown since 1783 and a glider had been demonstrated by George Cayley in 1853, it was not until 1874 that the French demonstrated an engine-powered aircraft. The box kite, invented by Australia's Lawrence Hargrave, received a new wing design in 1892. This facilitated later developments including the plane flown by the Wright brothers in North Carolina in 1903, the first sustained and controlled air flight. In 1909 George Taylor made the first Australian 'heavier than air flight' at Narrabeen, New South Wales, and powered flights soon followed in the other States. Four-engine planes were in the air by 1913, their development hastened by the threat of war.

1 *Possum-Hunting In The Future* (Sullivan, *Bulletin*, 1914). The possibilities of the new inventions seemed endless, especially to the outback humorist.

2 *"On The Girders"* (*Melbourne Punch*, 1913). The first aeroplanes were introduced just as skyscrapers were beginning to appear.

3 *Aerial Communication* (*Sydney Punch*, 1865). An earlier colonial flight of fancy is suggested by Giffard's trip in a steam-powered flying machine over Paris in 1852 at nine kilometres an hour.

4 *The Fall Of Man* (*Bulletin*, 1914). An early aviator is stranded after his plane runs aground on a chimney stack in a fanciful warning from a sceptical cartoonist.

5 *Fly for Pekin* (Unsigned, undated, *Rex Nan Kivell Collection*). A variety of transport—including 'aeroplanes' bound for New Zealand, Peking and Greenland, a parachute for Mexico and a balloon —stand ready to convey transcontinental travellers.

1

'POSSUM-HUNTING IN THE FUTURE.

2

"ON THE GIRDERS."

Bill.—"Them aireyoplanes don't seem hardly safe to me some ow."

Tom. "Yus. Wot I says is good ole' 'terrer firmer' for me."

3

AERIAL COMMUNICATION.

THIS IS A BEAUTIFUL FLIGHT OF FANCY.

4

THE FALL OF MAN.

Here endeth the first lesson.

5

1885–1925
Taking to the Water

The hot Australian summers eventually melted the rigid restrictions concerning bathing that were imported with the English. It was difficult to prohibit public bathing between six in the morning and eight in the evening as decreed in 1833, because that was the period when people most needed to cool off. Following 'protest' swims by Sydney newspaper editor William Gacher at Manly the laws were relaxed in 1903 to allow all-day bathing as long as 'neck-to-knee' costumes were worn. Surfboard riding, which began in Hawaii hundreds of years ago, had impressed Captain Cook in the 1770s. It became very popular in the United States and Australia around the turn of the century.

1 *"On The Jewelled Margin Of The Sea"* (Souter, *Bulletin*, 1905). Inevitably, the beach became a place to 'see and be seen', opening the way for the new bathing costumes industry.

2 *A New Industry* (*Melbourne Punch*, 1911). It was initially proposed that members of the Sydney Police Force should be recruited by the surf clubs to patrol the main beaches in case of accidents.

3 *A Little Suggestion* (Hop, *Bulletin*, 1885). The first surf-lifesaver, or a 'beach holiday policeman of Bondi', was created by Hop to take care of brawling holidaymakers who caused trouble.

4 *The Surfers' Tophet* (Brown, *Bulletin*, 1914). A Sydney paper claimed 'the garbage nuisance on the Manly beaches now includes decayed fruit and vegetables and dead animals including dogs and cats, which have strewn the ocean beach from end to end'.

5 *Merely A Matter Of Tense* (*Smith's Weekly*, 1925). Early surfboards were made of balsa, tapered at both ends, and were three metres long, eight centimetres thick and weighed at least ten kilos.

1

"ON THE JEWELLED MARGIN OF THE SEA."

HER: *"Aren't we too far out?"*
HIM: *"No, it's quite safe."*
HER: *"Very likely; but people can't see what we've got on."*

2

A NEW INDUSTRY

3

A Little Suggestion.

4

THE SURFERS' TOPHET.

5

MERELY A MATTER OF TENSE.
"Haven't I met you somewhere before?"
"Er—no—I don't think so."
"Then I'll meet you on the beach after."

1905–1913
Fancy Fashions: What Next?

Fashions of the period included the hobble skirt, which was long and gathered in around the ankles, and the harem scarem skirt, which bellowed out in the middle. Cartoonists, often misinterpreting female imitation of male dress, satirized women's attempts to be both comfortable and 'à la mode'. Perhaps the most outrageous garment of the pre-war period, however, was the bathing costume, which was not only worn out in the open on the main surfing beaches but was seen in such unlikely places as seaside railway stations. What indeed would happen next?

1 *Fair Game* (Minns, *Bulletin*, 1905). The cartoonist has a dig at both fashion and Aborigines here.

2 *The Mixed Sexes* (*Melbourne Punch*, 1911). A report on this 'harem scarem' skirt in a fashion journal claimed, 'There is a lot of witchery in the new garment', to which *Punch* replied, 'We don't doubt it, but which is witch?'.

3 *The Girl Of To-morrow* (*Melbourne Punch*, 1911). Although the cartoonist was satirizing female clothing, it is obvious that it was, except for the hat, becoming more streamlined, and hence more comfortable to wear compared to earlier cumbersome fashions such as the bustle and the hooped skirt.

4 *The Coming Costume* (Nuttall, *Melbourne Punch*, 1913). The daring brevity of the bathing costumes shocked the more modest members of the community, who instigated a movement aimed at forbidding such improper displays in public.

1

2

FAIR GAME.

"Where did you get your wife, Jimmy?"

"Caught her in the scrub."

THE MIXED SEXES.

3

THE GIRL OF TO-MORROW.

4

CHAPTER V

What Did You Do in the Great War, Daddy? 1914–1918

The Horrors of War
Museum of Frightfulness
Over the Top
The Girl He Left Behind
This Little Pig Stayed at Home
When Billjim Comes Marching Home
Fancy Fashions: What Next?

CHAPTER V
What Did You Do in the Great War, Daddy? 1914–1918

Returned 'diggers'

There were earlier wars in which Australians had been involved, but the Great War was the first in which the effort was national. The Boer War and other skirmishes before it had attracted contingents from the various colonies, but with Britain's declaration of war on Germany in August 1914 the new nation had a Prime Minister, Joseph Cook, who could say on behalf of all the States: 'If there is to be a war then you and I will be in it. We must be in it. If the Old Country is at war so are we'.

There were mixed feelings in Australia about the war. On the one hand, the conscription debates of 1916 and 1917 divided the country, but on the other the great displays of courage at Gallipoli and on the Somme gave Australians a sense of pride. They had jumped into adulthood overnight with their brave demonstration of loyalty. It was a costly example, for 7 600 died at Gallipoli. But out of the ashes came a national day and a memory which, for many years, bound the new nation.

Australia's enthusiasm for war was that of a young country springing to the aid of its ageing parent. More than 400 000 enlisted from a population of less than five million, and the first contingents arrived in Egypt within weeks of the declaration of war. It was only when news of the losses was reported that this zeal abated. With offensives such as the Somme, where 28 000 perished, the death toll rose quickly and before the end of the war 60 000, or one in five recruits, lay dead on foreign battlefields.

To many, the war was not Australia's affair, and for them life went on as usual. As the Sydney magazine *Australian Bystander* pointed out: 'Since the War the swarms of people taking to the surf at weekends are larger than ever, not one less game of cricket has been played, not a picture show, not a vaudeville has been closed because of the War; no pubs have closed, no race clubs have held fewer meetings; there is not a motorcar less in the street; concerts, entertainments and side shows have in fact increased in numbers and the beer and whisky trade is very brisk'.

Certainly, patriotic women nailed bleeding fowls to the front doors of 'eligibles' who refused to volunteer; the Australian League of Honour launched a 'thrift campaign' to 'avoid waste for the Empire' as a matter of extreme national importance; a Necessary Commodities Commission determined the price of necessary foodstuffs, commodities and services; 6 700 German nationals were interned; and women closed the ranks to fill jobs left vacant by departing volunteers and serve on the Australian Red Cross. But although patriotic composers may have been writing rousing military music, and poets turned out stirring ballads, there were many who turned their backs on the European war.

The themes that preoccupied the cartoonists included the new style of warfare and the suffering of innocent victims. Thousands died in the European theatre, where diseases and starvation added to the carnage of conflict. The trench humour of the digger helped him to survive the ordeal and gave the nation a new brand of jokes. The cartoonists felt for the girls who had been left behind but criticized the shirker who stayed at home rather than 'doing his bit' at the front. According to the cartoonists the mood of the country had been changed considerably by the war.

During these years, the *Bulletin* faced vigorous competition from the emerging working man's papers for dominance in the field of cartooning. The *Australian Worker* challenged the older, established newspaper much in the same way as the *Bulletin* had earlier defied *Punch*. The challenge was short-lived, however, and the changing social climate after the war threw up another rival, *Smith's Weekly*.

The figure which had hitherto represented Australia was deposed during the war. The sulky Little Boy from Manly was suddenly way out of his time, an anachronism; he belonged to the comparatively innocent Victorian era. The slaughter at Gallipoli dressed his successor in a uniform and put him in a trench. Certainly there were images of softer anti-conscriptionist Australians, but the predominant identity by 1918 was the returned digger who looked everyone squarely in the eye, anticipating respect. For he was one who had no hesitation in answering the inevitable question '*What Did You Do In The Great War, Daddy?*'.

The 'shirker' who would not go

1914–1918
The Horrors of War

The Great War brought suffering to millions of non-combatants. Life may have gone on much as before in Australia, but in Europe the stories of German atrocities inspired sacrifices by the patriotic. The German armies ploughed through the continent leaving a trail of destruction behind them. Their terrifying aircraft bombed towns and their gunboats and mines sank neutral ships along with the enemy's. Blockades, trade 'blacklists' and interrupted supply lines caused widespread hunger. Governments controlled vital industries and rationed bread, meat and butter but many perished as a result of the starvation and disease that swept Europe in the wake of the 'Hun machine'.

1 *"Onward Christian Soldiers!"* (Lindsay, *Bulletin*, 1915). Despite their profession of Christian faith, the invading German soldiers killed women and children along with civilians and introduced the deadly poisonous gas.

2 *Kultur For The Blind* (Lindsay, *Bulletin*, 1918). The Germans attacked a number of neutral British ships early in the war, including the *Lusitanià*, which was sunk in 1915 with the loss of 1 198 lives. Hospital ships such as this one, the *Warilda*, received torpedo hits which made it 'impossible to succour the blinded men who groped about in the darkness in the swirling waters until they drowned'.

3 *Blocking An Ally* (Low, *Bulletin*, 1916). Many German civilians starved during the war because of trade boycotts that prevented essential foodstuffs from reaching them.

4 *The Red Ploughman Of Europe* (Lindsay, *Bulletin*, 1916). The huge number of civilian deaths inspired cartoonists such as Lindsay to offer their talents to the government's recruiting drives.

5 *The Non-Combatants* (Low, *Bulletin*, 1914). Millions of refugees were driven from their homes by the war to die from starvation on the trail.

1

"ONWARD, CHRISTIAN SOLDIERS!"

2

3

BLOCKING AN ALLY.

4

THE RED PLOUGHMAN OF EUROPE.

5

THE NON-COMBATANTS.

1914–1916
Museum of Frightfulness

Science, too, was enlisted in the service of warfare and shocked many of the onlookers who were the first generation to witness technology used for such inhuman purposes. Zeppelins attacked London in 1915 and aircraft of various designs were dropping bombs on many European capitals by the end of the war. Poison gas was introduced in 1915, tanks were used for the first time in 1916, and at sea, concealed mines and submarines lay waiting for enemy vessels. These modern weapons had a sobering effect on the sabre-waving Australians who had so eagerly dashed into war on the trusty stock-horses that had served them well in South Africa.

1 *Awake, Arise!* (Lindsay, *Bulletin*, 1914). In a pre-war defence report Britain's General Ian Hamilton warned, 'Australia must aim to be mistress of her own air as she is of her land and sea'.

2 *The Campaign Of Frightfulness* (Hop, *Bulletin*, 1916). Germans try to drop bombs on Australian Prime Minister Billy 'Win the War' Hughes, during his European pep talk tour.

3 *The Puzzled Square-Head* (Lindsay, *Bulletin*, 1916). The Hun asks the world why it is so critical of him when he has 'enriched civilization with all these new and beautiful ideas'.

4 *Wonders Of Science!* (Dyson, *Daily Herald*, 1915). The application of the new aeroplane to warfare was inevitable and immediate: London was bombed in 1915.

5 *Times and Changes* (Low, *Bulletin*, 1914). Old-style warfare gives way to modern horrors and the digger dives for cover. Fifty years before it had been 'let me like a soldier fall!'; now it became 'let me like a soldier crawl'.

1

AWAKE, ARISE!

THE BOY: "I reckon, old bird, you'll have to learn to fly."

2

THE CAMPAICN CF FRIGHTFULNESS.

3

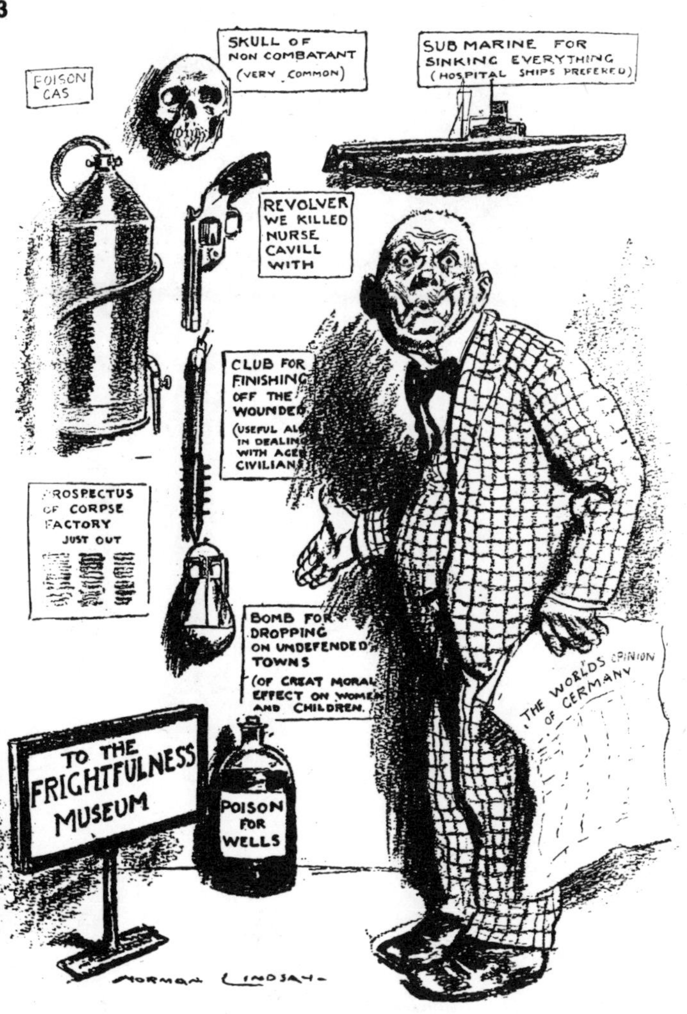

THE PUZZLED SQUARE-HEAD.

4

WONDERS OF SCIENCE!

5

TIMES AND CHANGES.

1913–1918
Over the Top

An Australian digger wrote back from the front line in 1916 saying, 'It is this saving grace of humour that makes life worth living here at Gallipoli; but it also makes the Ghurkas and Tommies wonder what manner of men we are. The Englishmen regard the Gallipoli campaign with great seriousness, the Indians appear stoically indifferent, the Australians regard the whole show as a great adventure'. In this vein the diggers played cricket and football on the beach, sometimes in view of the Turkish snipers, and devised a series of front line games to while away the time. Jokes abounded and many trickled back to those at home to enrich the Australian tradition.

1 *Rebuked* (Minns, *Bulletin*, 1918). The lack of respect for authority or social class gave Australian soldiers an egalitarian image that was envied by troops from countries with more hierarchical traditions.

2 *Two-up* (Nuttal, *Melbourne Punch*, 1918). The diggers never lost their passion for gambling, even when under enemy fire.

3 *The Jester At The Court Of Mars* (Lindsay, *Bulletin*, 1916). Contrary to all traditions of warfare, the Australian digger enters the theatre with a sense of humour.

1

2

3

THE JESTER AT THE COURT OF MARS.

1916–1918
The Girl He Left Behind

The Great War brought emotions to the surface as never before. With 400 000 young men enlisting there were thousands of sweethearts and wives left behind; with 60 000 dying there were thousands bereaved; with 200 000 wounded there were thousands distressed. And with the debate over conscription there were thousands who were confused and uncertain of how to feel. For every poet that warned, 'I hear his widow cry in the night, I hear his children weep', there was another writing, 'he had taken down the sliprails and set the mustered cattle free, he had kissed his sobbing sweetheart by the moonlit wilga tree, and had turned his trusty stockhorse towards the great melee'.

1 *A Final Request* (Colahan, *Bulletin*, 1916). The serious topic of war did not prevent cartoonists from deriving humour at women's expense.

2 *The New Recruiting Campaign* (Minns, *Bulletin*, 1917). Married men were less likely to be criticized than single men for not volunteering.

3 *Chance To Keep His Hand In* (Listed, *Bulletin*, 1918). Cartoonists have always found a place for mother-in-law jokes, even during the war.

4 *For His Encouragement* (Butler, *Bulletin*, 1916). The marriage rate skyrocketed as young soldiers sought a partner before departing for the front.

5 *The Complete Warrior* (Minns, *Bulletin*, 1917). The legends of Anzac courage were fuelled with boasts such as this.

6 *Dead On* (Souter, *Bulletin*, 1917). The harsh realities of the war forced a relaxation of strict moral codes, introducing an era of permissiveness that reached its height in the 1920s.

1

A FINAL REQUEST.
"And, dearest, promise me if you win a V.C. that you won't go and give it to some other girl for a hatpin."

2

B E MINNS

THE NEW RECRUITING CAMPAIGN.
"Marry me, marry me, darling, and save me."

3

CHANCE TO KEEP HIS HAND IN.

THE HERO: *"I wonder if I shall be able to settle down to the peaceful home life after four years of the horrors of war?"*

HIS FIANCEE: *"Of course we can have dear mother for a day or two at any time."*

4

FOR HIS ENCOURAGEMENT.

THE LASS: *"You're so—so different to the other boys."*

THE LAD (*flattered*): *"Really! In what way?"*

THE LASS: *"Well—er—they are always pestering me to marry them."*

5

THE COMPLETE WARRIOR.

"And have you really and truly killed a lot of Germans."

"Cert! Why, when we went over the top I always carried a scythe-stone to touch up me bayonet when it got blunt."

6

DEAD ON.

"Would you scream if I kissed you?"

"I don't see how I can if you kiss me on the right place."

1917–1918 This Little Pig Stayed at Home

Because of the massacres that were taking place on the front, great resentment was felt towards those who had not enlisted. It was felt that the losses would not have been so large had there been more volunteers, and in the eyes of the patriots, those who stayed behind shared the guilt for the death of their fallen comrades. But these 'shirkers' could not be moved, as the defeated conscription referenda of 1916 and 1917 demonstrated. It was not their war and as the IWW, or 'Wobblies', had shown, workers across national boundaries often had more in common with each other than they had with the profiteers from their own country who were making money from the conflict.

1 *Shameless* (Lindsay, *Bulletin*, 1918). The person who had not enlisted, and who therefore suffered none of the ravages of war, was made to feel extremely guilty by the proliferation of such cartoons as this.

2 *This Little Pig Stayed At Home* (Marquet, *Australian Worker*, 1917). For many the war represented merely good business as the price of scarce commodities rose and the interruption of normal market forces widened the scope for the cunning entrepreneur.

3 *Drunks* (Lindsay, *Bulletin*, 1917). The war did little to deter the drinkers back home and drunkenness reached such proportions during the war that a campaign was initiated to restrict drinking hours for those who had not volunteered to fight.

1

SHAMELESS.

2

THIS LITTLE PIG STAYED AT HOME.

DRUNKS

At times the world goes on the jag
 And Bacchus reigns supreme,
While through the city's carnival
 There pass, in giddy stream,
The talking drunk, the laughing drunk,
 The drunk who plans out wars,
The splendid drunk—the man of wealth
 Who orders motor-cars.

I meet them all, and grip their hands;
 We have a drink or so;
But, suddenly, I find myself
 With others that I know—
The sporting drunk, the old-pal drunk
 I have not met for years,
The joking drunk, the sleeping drunk,
 The drunk who gives loud cheers.

The masque is brisk; the sober drunk
 Who knows when he should cease
Quick-changes to the fighting drunk,
 Whose argument is peace;
Or else, becomes the bitter drunk
 Who leads an awful life,
And talks of suicide and prawns,
 Hate tram-rides and his wife.

The whole wide, sober-minded world
 Seems out upon the spree;
And every drunk in all the crowd
 Insists on drinks with me;
The crayfish drunk, the smart-man drunk
 Who tales of swindle springs,
The drunk whose father was a lord,
 The drunk who gaily sings.

The drunk who loved a thousand girls,
 The drunk who would be fed;
The laughing drunk; the mournful drunk
 Who glories in the dead;
The drunk who skips; the drunk who shouts
 For strange and awful food;
The boxing drunk; the penitent
 Who—once—was very good!

It's ten to one when I awake
 Upon some singing shore,
From visions of assorted drunks
 Who talk, laugh, sing and roar,
A stray drunk waves a bottle high
 And shouts, in cheery tones,
About the splendid time we've had—
 A drunk whose name is Jones.

1916–1918
When Billjim Comes Marching Home

It had been a long drawn-out war and when news of the Armistice reached Australia there was pandemonium. Crowds poured into city centres where they linked arms and danced and sang into the small hours of the morning. Drink flowed freely, musicians appeared from nowhere and speakers leapt up to congratulate the allies, attack the Hun and amuse the crowds generally. Described as 'patriotic hooliganism' by startled authorities, the crowd's behaviour sometimes got out of hand. For example, in Melbourne tram cars were derailed and shop windows broken. In Sydney and other towns around Australia there were similar scenes of rowdy celebrations. By the time the soldiers came back, however, the festive mood had subsided and many diggers returned unnoticed to a workaday world that was back to normal.

1 *The Best Of All Christmas Boxes—Big Brother Bill Comes Home* (Lindsay, *Bulletin*, 1918). As one in five who enlisted were killed in the Great War, those who came home were greeted with unrestrained joy by their families.

2 *The Horrors Of War* (Lindsay, *Bulletin*, 1916). The tales of the war were many and varied.

3 *The Truce* (Lindsay, *Bulletin*, 1918). The war ends at last with Bacchus and Death sharing a cigar and a tankard of beer.

4 *More Horrors Of War* (Souter, *Bulletin*, 1918). After many years apart couples inevitably found it difficult to fall back into step again.

1

THE BEST OF ALL CHRISTMAS BOXES—BIG BROTHER BILL COMES HOME

2

THE HORRORS OF WAR.

GALLIPOLI BILL: *"Terrible experiences out there! My oath we had! Why, a bloke in Egypt sold me two bottles o' salt water for beer!"*

THE TRUCE.

4

MORE HORRORS OF WAR.

"She seems very cut up."

"Yes, poor thing. She had bad news from France yesterday. Her husband is coming home on the next boat."

1916–1919
Fancy Fashions: What Next?

The social upheaval of the Great War completely changed fashion. The enforced shortages had stripped away the pretensions and emancipated women, who began to wear simple, free-hanging clothes. Contemporary fashions certainly included remnants such as hatpins and bonnets of the Victorian and Edwardian eras, but after women had worked in essential, wartime industries where they had worn standardized clothing, it no longer seemed appropriate to dress up in the extravagant garments once so popular. Thus the way was cleared for the daring simplicity of the 1920s fashions.

1 *Looking Ahead* (Minns, *Bulletin*, 1916). While their husbands risked their lives at the front, the ladies of society continued to parade their fashions.

2 *Two Chances* (Souter, *Bulletin*, 1916). Dressing to show off was considered poor form by many during the war, especially the older generation.

3 *"Terrible war—isn't it?"* (Souter, *Bulletin*, 1916). Those who merely danced the war away were referred to by the patriotic as the 'pleasure as usual brigade'.

4 *Other Beaches, Other Costumes* (Souter, *Bulletin*, 1916). It was during the Great War that the 'neck to knee costume complete with modest skirt' gave way to such brief garments as this.

5 *The Dawn Of Peace* (Marquet, *Australian Worker*, 1918). 11 November, 1918, brought a cessation of hostilities in Europe and gave the young Australian nation an opportunity to grow and develop in a long day of peace.

6 *Beauty Unadorned* (Low, *Bulletin*, 1919). The war worked wonders for some.

1

LOOKING AHEAD.

MRS. JONES: "Doesn't Mrs. Golightly dress with more than her usual style and good taste of late?"

MRS. SMART: "Ah, you see, my dear, her husband's regiment is in the very front of the firing line."

2

TWO CHANCES.

"Do you think your husband will care to see you in that costume?"

"If he doesn't, somebody else's may."

3

"Terrible war—isn't it?"
"Frightful—why this is the seventh Red Cross Dance I've been to this week!"

4

OTHER BEACHES, OTHER COSTUMES.
Anzac v. Bondi.

5

THE DAWN OF PEACE.

6

BEAUTY UNADORNED.
BLOSSOM: *"What a grimly determined, pugnacious looking and masterful man Major Fitzdoodle is!"*
ROSEBUD: *"Camouflage, my dear, mere camouflage! You didn't know the Major before the war."*

CHAPTER VI

When Dad and Dave Were Down and Out 1919–1938

CHAPTER VI
When Dad and Dave Were Down and Out 1919–1938

Dad and Dave

The period between the two wars was one of great disillusionment in Australia. Having had great hopes for their country, hopes which they fought for with great valour, the returning diggers were disappointed to find that it was unable to offer them the kind of home they felt they deserved. The economic and social climate had changed, and despite the terrible sacrifices the diggers had made, it was not a land fit for heroes. In 1922, the State funeral of the romantic nationalist Henry Lawson seemed to symbolize the death of Australian idealism.

Disappointment, then, was the mood portrayed by the cartoonists of the 1920s and 1930s as they took on the role of conscience of the nation. The promises of the leaders who had exhorted men to enlist were not kept after the war. What the Anzacs had fought for was not forthcoming. Instead of the idealism that had once inspired the nation, there was now a feeling of desperate apprehension. There was barely time to replace the losses of the first war before the downhill slide into depression and war engulfed the country once again.

'What had it all been for?' was a question often asked in the cartoons of the interwar period. The Hun had not really been stopped, freedom did not guarantee a job, let alone a square meal, public health was threatened by outbreaks of influenza and polio, and the nation was often bitterly divided as strikers first battled with the police and then with the New Guard which sprang up to reflect the forces of reaction in the troubled 1930s. As social conditions deteriorated there were food riots, violent demonstrations and an increasing incidence of crime. Communism terrified many, and the assisted migrants who poured in from Britain under the 'men, money and markets' programme infuriated those unable to find work for themselves.

But, as the cartoons indicate, the depression was not only economic. The spirit of the community—still mourning its dead and unable to feed its young—sank to an all-time low. Morale was bound to fall when many were reduced to living in shanty towns, sleeping in humpies, scavenging around garbage bins and begging for food at railway stations. Without jobs they could not pay the rent, and as a consequence many families constructed makeshift huts near the point where their weekly sustenance cheque was paid out.

Thus, returning from the war, many needed to escape and found solace in the bottle. Frustrations were vented in the wild drinking and dancing spree that was later dubbed 'the roaring twenties'. Prohibition movements fought in vain to stamp out drinking, for people now wanted desperately to have a good time, amusing themselves with the 'talkies', the radio, the motor car and the aeroplane. The party, however, was not to last long, and within ten years of the end of the war, the bubble had burst and the glitter was gone. The depression struck.

It is no coincidence that the figures which emerged to represent Australians in this period were Dad and Dave. There was a retreat to the bush after the harsh realities of the war; it was thought that only in the back-blocks could a truly Australian identity be forged anew. If they were to cope with their deprivations, people needed a sense of humour that would allow them to transform their problems into something they could laugh at.

As if to meet this demand, *Smith's Weekly* jumped onto centre stage offering a new brand of bush jokes, tailor-made for the diggers. The paper was so successful during the interwar period that it dislodged the *Bulletin* from its throne and, along with daily newspapers, set a cheekier and more irreverent tone that suited a generation which felt it had been wronged.

As it was, the idealism in the face of the returned digger quickly turned to the angry impatience of the hard-bitten workmen of the 1930s, who came to symbolize Australians up to the outbreak of World War II. The crash was inevitable. The euphoria that accompanied Federation could not be sustained, and the suffering created by the war and, not long after, the depression, had bred a new type. Australia and Australians could never be the same again. Such were the effects of those nightmare days, *When Dad and Dave Were Down and Out*.

Australians of the thirties

1919–1931
Land Fit For Heroes

Australia was a sick country when the diggers returned. Influenza epidemics imported from Europe hospitalized many and claimed the lives of 11 552 between 1918 and 1922. The benefits of repatriation turned out to be grossly inadequate. The Soldier Settlement Scheme was inappropriate for diggers with city backgrounds and their consequent mismanagement led them to ruin. Wholesale prices were more than double pre-war levels. Diggers found jobs difficult to obtain and because many of those who had stayed at home had opposed Australian involvement in the war, the diggers were often met with indifference rather than sympathy. In 1920 the Returned Serviceman's League was formed to champion the cause of the forgotten soldiers.

1 *Her House In Disorder* (Danelly, *Bulletin*, 1919). After four years of continual warfare there was much to be done before the order of pre-war life could be re-established.

2 *No Man's land* (Virgil, *Smith's Weekly*, 1931). Before long the horrors of war were replaced by those of peace and many diggers felt it was like being back at the front—except there, at least, they received their daily rations.

3 *Repatriated* (Low, *Bulletin*, 1919). The soldier settler schemes aimed at rewarding Anzacs with a block of land, but with an unfavourable economic conditions, an erratic climate and limited farming experience, the digger often failed to make ends meet.

4 *The Arrest* (Low, *Bulletin*, 1919). The influenza epidemic that claimed 11 552 lives was finally brought under control in 1920.

5 *What's In A Name?* (Finey, *Smith's Weekly*, 1930). Maimed soldiers had little but memories to sustain them. Work was unavailable and government pensions were less than half the basic wage even for diggers who had lost both legs.

6 *"Nothing's Too Good For The Soldier"* (Leason, *Bulletin*, 1921). In a labour market where there were more applicants than vacancies, disabled soldiers were passed over for able-bodied men.

1

HER HOUSE IN DISORDER.

2

NO MAN'S LAND

3

REPATRIATED.

4

THE ARREST.

5

WHAT'S IN A NAME?

6

"NOTHING'S TOO GOOD FOR THE SOLDIER."

1919–1925
Migrant Sewage

Under the Empire Settlement Act of 1922 Australia agreed to co-operate in an immigration assistance scheme aimed at relieving Britain of its surplus unemployed and providing the less populated country with more men for labour and defence. The population was only six million in 1925 and with the threat of Japan to the north most Australians favoured enlarging the reservoir of armed forces. But since there were not enough jobs to go around, few welcomed migrants who could displace them from the workforce. As they often worked harder for smaller wages, the newcomers were inevitably resented and discriminated against.

1 *White Australia* (Cross, *Smith's Weekly*, 1919). At the Versailles Peace Conference, Australian Prime Minister, Billy Hughes, upheld the 'White Australia' policy by stubbornly holding out against a racial equality clause sponsored by Japan.

2 *A Scottish Suicide Club—Or Economy At Dunedin* (Waring, *Smith's Weekly*, 1925). The Scottish migrants featured in many bigoted jokes of the period.

3 *Another Dirt Plague* (Finey, *Smith's Weekly*, 1925). The first Yugoslavs to arrive in the interwar period met with considerable discrimination.

4 *"What's th' Pommy do?"* (Nuvel, *Smith's Weekly*, 1925). The large post-war English immigration programme was resented by workers and provided cartoonists with innumerable racist jokes.

5 *Some Presents from Uncle Jozif* (Finey, *Smith's Weekly*, 1923). Australia's lack of population appeared dangerous in the face of large numbers of immigrants, who were often likened to a plague of rats.

1

WHITE AUSTRALIA

2

A Scottish Suicide Club—or Economy at Dunedin.

3

Another Dirt Plague

4

"What's th' Pommy do when 'e's finished milkin'?"
"Drinks th' flamin' milk."

5

Some Presents From Uncle Jozif

1922—1938 Dad and Dave Dine Out

Although many characters evolved in the cartoons of the day, Dad and Dave became the most popular. By the late 1920s they had assumed the identities of real people; readers followed their exploits with devotion, and many stories, jokes and radio plays were written about them. It was an age in which the simple innocence of the outback was treasured and Dad and Dave answered not only the need to have truly Australian characters in the folklore of the day, but to have characters who could cheer people up. The outback father and son team remained popular until they became irrelevant to the urban culture of the 1960s.

1 *Dad: "Wait 'ere till I go an' see"* (Cross, *Smith's Weekly*, 1925). Like most of their countrymen Dad and Dave were down and out during the interwar period and lucky if they could afford a square meal.

2 *Parson: And they threw Joseph into the Pit* (Jonsson, *Smith's Weekly*, 1930). In an age when the influence of the Church was rapidly declining, Dad and Dave were often used to portray those backblocks Australians who were beyond salvation.

3 *"Tired, Dad? Care For The Saddle?"* (Cross, *Smith's Weekly*, 1931). Dave has another bright idea for his Dad, who is never more at home than when in the saddle.

4 *Dave: Hey! Which bed we gonner say our prayers against?* (Cross, *Smith's Weekly*, 1938). After the wild drinking and dancing of the roaring twenties the simple innocence of Dave came as a welcome relief.

5 *Boss: "What you doin' out here, Jacky?"* (Cross, *Smith's Weekly*, 1922). Jacky, the Aboriginal station hand, was another outback character who helped many laugh during the interwar period.

1

Dad: "Wait 'ere till I go in an' see wot they want for their dinners. I'll coo-ee, if it's only a bob."

2

PARSON: And they threw Joseph into the pit.
DAD: That's the only way they'll get these flamin' miners to work.

3

STAN CROSS

"TIRED, DAD? CARE FOR THE SADDLE?"

4

DAVE: Hey! Which bed we gonner say our prayers against?

5

Boss: "What you doin' out here, Jacky? The wood's under the shed!"
Jacky: "Roof's too low, boss—mine swing-it axe out here an' run in quick an' hit him."

1930–1933
No Jobs for the Boys

Economic conditions had been deteriorating since the end of the war but when the great depression hit Australia in 1929, businesses collapsed overnight, throwing thousands out of work. Because of its dependence on overseas loans and the sale of primary produce, Australia was badly affected. With the fall in export prices and the evaporation of capital, there was little consumer spending. The basic wage was slashed by 10 per cent in an effort to keep up employment but by 1932 30 per cent of the workforce was out of work. Shops closed, homes were vacated by tenants who could not afford to pay the rent and a large number of men took to the roads to scavenge for food and work.

1 *But what of the enemy WITHIN, who is ravaging our country NOW?* (Donald, *Australian Worker*, 1933). By 1929 unemployment had reached 19 per cent, by 1931 it was 27 per cent and in 1932 it peaked at 30 per cent of the workforce. To many it was a greater threat than any enemy abroad.

2 *Co-operation* (Percival, *Bulletin*, 1933). Thousands left the cities to search in vain for work in the bush. Jobs were so scarce that men could tramp hundreds of kilometres before finding even a day's casual labour.

3 *Does Mars Stage A Come-Back For The Next Year* (Dunne, *Smith's Weekly*, 1931). It was feared by many that the world financial crisis would lead to war.

4 *Basic Wage* (Finey, *Labor Daily*, 1930). Reduced in 1930 the basic wage was again cut—this time by 10 per cent—in February 1931.

1

But what of the enemy WITHIN, who is ravaging our country NOW?

2

CO-OPERATION.
THE BAGMAN: *"Any chance of a job about here, Boss?"*
THE BOSS: *"Well, you could come in with one of us cockies and go fifty-fifty in what we ain't makin'."*

3

4

TEA AND CAKES ONE SHILLING

Basic Wage

1922–1930
Taking to the Bottle

When prohibition was introduced in the United States in 1920 it became illegal to manufacture, sell or buy alcoholic drinks. It lasted until 1933 when, because of the abuses, the law was repealed. Drinking had undermined social life in Australia to such an extent during this time that strong pressure was exerted to introduce prohibition laws down under. In 1926 prohibitionists boasted that they would 'eliminate all traffic in liquor in Australia even if it meant bloodshed!'. When the referenda on the question were put, however, the people voted to retain their right to drink. The American example had clearly shown how difficult it was to enforce prohibition laws and how dangerous the speak-easies of the bootleggers could be.

1 *Inebriated One* (Hartt, *Smith's Weekly*, 1922). Drinking was so common in the interwar period that jokes about drunks achieved a record popularity in the journals of the day.

2 *Greetings* (Leason, *Bulletin*, 1927). As congregations declined and the Church lost its influence over people, a novel scheme was suggested to increase its audience.

3 *"Memories Of 1918"* (Finey, *Smith's Weekly*, 1929). For the forgotten diggers, drinking was the most forgivable of sins.

4 *Walking Out Together!* (Leason, *Bulletin*, 1930). The bootleggers encouraged the Temperance Societies to ban drinking so that they could make their fortunes selling liquor through the illegal speak-easies.

5 *"Did I Hear That Gong Again"* (Litchfield, *Bulletin*, 1926). The leaders of the Temperance Societies declared war on drink, claiming it was at least partially responsible for the moral decay of the 1920s.

1

Inebriated One (to Railway Signalman): "I'll 'ave a (hic) pint a' beer, pleash."

2

GREETINGS.

3

"MEMORIES OF 1918"

Eleventh day of eleventh month,
Eleven years ago;
And now I wait for eleven strokes
From the tower of the G.P.O.

The hours have run and the days are done.
When mud was the daily life,
Of the lads in France, while the heat-whirls' dance,
Was theirs in the desert strife.

Nights that were mad with the snarling shell,
Nights that were eerie cold;
Nights when we tried to forget the hell—
Though the distant guns still rolled.

Noons when we marched with our arms reversed,
As hospitals spewed their dead;
Noons when our cobber raved and cursed—
Christ! How the poor cow bled!

Dug-outs and boots and the brazier's smoke,
I think I can smell them yet ....
Perhaps that's why I seem to choke
At the thought of the mates I met.

What does it matter who won the war?
If out of the fire of pain
The soldier stands to the vows he swore,
"It shall not happen again!"

But the hours have run and the days are done,
When mud was the daily life
Of the lads in France, while the heat-whirls' dance
Was theirs in the desert strife.

Eleventh day of eleventh month,
Eleven years ago!
I stand as I wait for eleven strokes
From the tower of the G.P.O.

—*Geoffrey Cumine.*

4

Walking Out Together!

"ENGAGEMENTS"

5

"DID I HEAR THAT GONG AGAIN?"

1927–1937
The Roaring Twenties

The good times of 'the roaring twenties' were so intense that revellers must have harboured a premonition that there would only be this one brief fling before the inevitable crash. Australians needed to let their hair down to forget the terrible losses at the front, and the diversions of the age, such as drinking, smoking, talking pictures, jazz and dancing helped them to turn a blind eye to the economic and social problems that were fast engulfing their country.

1 *He: I believe they are going to wear them shorter next year* (*Smith's Weekly*, 1928). The briefer clothing of the day contributed to the atmosphere of social freedom which seemed to intoxicate the revellers.

2 *The Intruder* (Cross, *Smith's Weekly*, 1927). Kissing in public was frowned upon before the war but became the vogue during the roaring twenties.

3 *"Why did you object to him kissing you on the mat?"* (*Smith's Weekly*, 1930). Dancing girls, looking like early 'go-go' girls, were a popular feature of many entertainment halls.

4 *Lady (shocked): How gauche!* (Haiseman, *Smith's Weekly*, 1937). Heavy drinking was condoned by many at the endless parties where the term 'blotto' was born.

5 *The Pilgrim's Progress* (Lindsay, *Bulletin*, 1933). Whatever forces inspired the wowsers, they certainly made a valiant attempt to check the debauchery of the times.

1

HE: I believe they are going to wear them shorter next year.
SHE:- What?
HE: Trousers.

2

The Intruder: Excuse me, may I have the pleasure of the next?

3

"Why did you object to him kissing you on the mat?"
"It was the bathmat!"

4

LADY (shocked): How gauche!
BLOTTO: Fine, thanks, how goesh it with you?

5

THE PILGRIM'S PROGRESS.

1900–1932 The Reluctant Coathanger

Sydney waited a long time for its harbour bridge. It was first proposed in 1815 by convict architect Francis Greenway, who said, 'If a bridge were to be thrown across from Dawes Battery to the North Shore a town could be built over there'. His scheme, like many that followed it, came to nothing. There was the Henderson design of 1857; the 1878 floating bridge plan; the 1877 seven-span truss bridge design; the 1880 government scheme for a high level bridge; the 1901 New York company's submission for a cantilever bridge; the 1908 government twin tunnel plan for cars and trains and construction finally began on the long-awaited bridge in 1923. Nine years later it was completed.

1 *The North Shore Bridge* (Hop, *Bulletin*, 1900). Government officials considered almost every conceivable design for the bridge before settling on the suspension style.

2 *The Bridge—Everybody's Bridge* (Lindsay, *Bulletin*, 1914). Although the politicians of the day claimed credit when the original Bradfield design was selected, the ghosts of earlier planners, including Sir Henry Parkes and George Reid, returned to say the bridge idea was theirs.

3 *The First Girl To Walk Home Over The Bridge* (*Smith's Weekly*, 1932). Late night strolls across the bridge were full of hazards for single females.

4 *Said the Pup* (Miller, *Smith's Weekly*, 1932). Following an unscheduled opening of the bridge by Captain de Groot of the reactionary New Guard, the ceremony was officially performed by New South Wales Labor Premier Jack Lang on 19 March 1932.

5 *We've Started To Build Our North Shore Bridge* (Hallett, *Smith's Weekly*, 1925). After decades of discussing the designs and raising the finance, construction work began on the approaches to the bridge in April 1923.

1

THE NORTH SHORE BRIDGE.

2

THE BRIDGE—EVERYBODY'S BRIDGE.

3

4

SAID THE PUP: "Wonder if it's open for dogs yet?"

5

We've Started To Build Our North Shore Bridge

1927–1929
Car Crazy

Motor cars became so popular during the 1920s that the State governments were forced to pass legislation controlling their use. The first Traffic Act had been introduced in 1909 by the New South Wales government, which demanded that cars be registered and drivers obtain licences. These restrictions did not apply in other States for some time, however, because automobile associations considered restrictions to be an infringement of liberty. But as the cars got faster it became obvious that controls would have to be tighter. Early speed limits of four and then six miles an hour were imposed in the towns and licensing and registration were eventually introduced in all States. With 600 000 motorized vehicles in 1930, Australians had more cars per capita than any other country except America.

1 *Force Of Habit* (Miller, *Smith's Weekly*, 1929). The change-over from the horse was not always easy.

2 *Tragedy of the Flapper and the Backfire* (*Smith's Weekly*, 1929). The early cars were started by a crank-handle which could backfire with spectacular results.

3 *The Gentle Spirit of Traffic Congestion* (Finey, *Smith's Weekly*, 1928). It was not long before traffic congestion became a major problem in the cities.

4 *The Cave Man, 1928* (Leason, *Bulletin*, 1927). Early jokes about motor accidents soon gave way to horror as ever faster cars left a trail of unprecedented carnage.

5 *Australia Will Soon Have A Car To Every Family* (Finey, *Smith's Weekly*, 1928). The mass produced T-model Ford helped popularize the automobile in Australia and by the end of the 1920s the car had transformed travelling.

1

FORCE OF HABIT

2

Tragedy of the Flapper and the Backfire

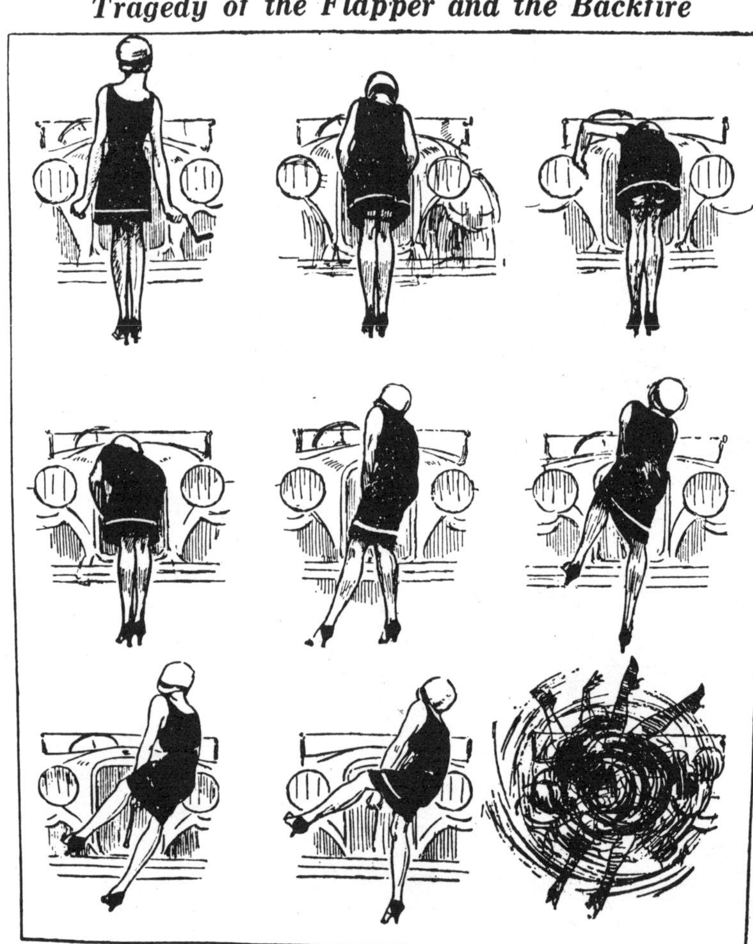

3

THE GENTLE SPIRIT OF TRAFFIC CONGESTION

He won't be happy till every mudguard in the Commonwealth has a dent in it.

4

THE CAVE MAN 1928

5

AUSTRALIA WILL SOON HAVE A CAR TO EVERY FAMILY

1919–1933
Trains and Planes

The problem of standardizing the rail gauges persisted long after the major cities were connected by rail and the completion of the trans-Australian railway in 1917. Each State held out for its own gauge and it was not until 1962 that Melbourne and Sydney were linked by standard gauge. More progress was being made in the air, however, and in 1919 the Smith brothers flew from England to Australia. The following year, QANTAS was established and Western Australia introduced an airmail service. In 1928 a Flying Doctor Service was inaugurated, Charles Kingsford Smith became the first person to fly across the Pacific ocean, and Hinkler and Ulm flew from London to Darwin in 129 hours. In 1931 the first Anglo-Australian airmail was carried, and by 1938 QANTAS was operating a European flying boat service.

1 *The Spirit of the Air* (Lindsay, *Bulletin*, 1933). Early air crashes were greeted with horror, and when Charles Kingsford Smith's aircraft disappeared over the Indian Ocean in 1935 the entire nation mourned.

2 *Exorcising The Australian Devil* (Lindsay, *Bulletin*, 1920). For many years parochialism prevented agreement on a standard rail gauge.

3 *The Future Of The Aeroplane* (Leason, *Bulletin*, 1919). As the achievements of the aeroplane grew, so did the number of fanciful suggestions for its future application.

1

THE SPIRIT OF THE AIR.

2

EXORCISING THE AUSTRALIAN DEVIL.

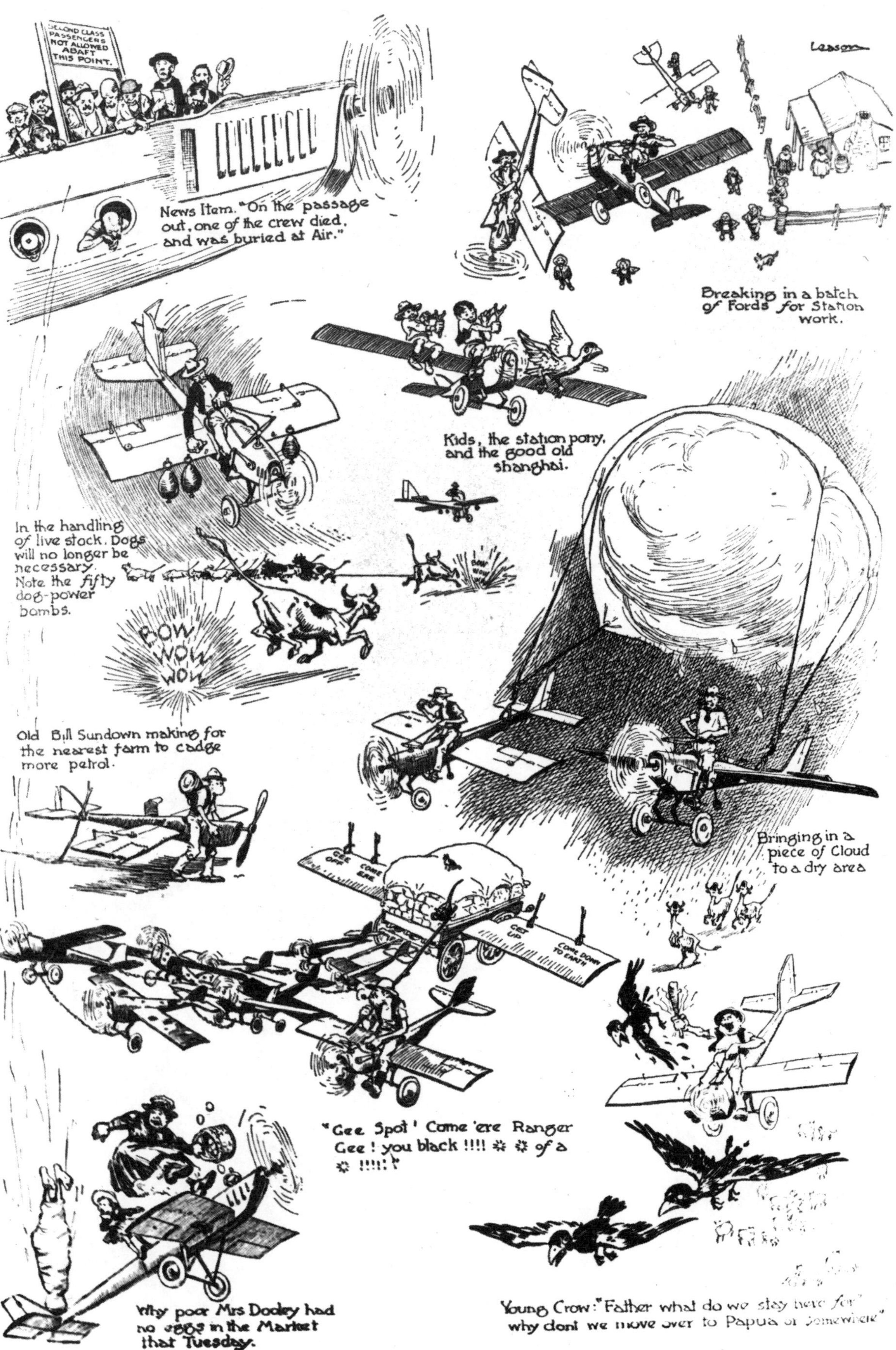

THE FUTURE OF THE AEROPLANE.

1927–1946
In (And On) the Air

Skyscrapers were radically changing the shape of the city skyline at the same time that 'talkies' and radio were enjoying unprecedented audiences. In 1920 there were only 720 cinemas all showing silent films but by the end of the period there were thousands of cinemas offering 'talkies'. The first regular radio broadcasts were transmitted in 1923. Within six months, 1 400 licences were taken out as people bought radio sets and 'the trains and ferries were buzzing with remarks bearing on the previous night's broadcasts'. The Australian Broadcasting Commission was formed in 1932 and by 1937 one million radio licences had been taken out.

1 *Sky Scrapers and the Saint* (Hallett, *Smith's Weekly*, 1927). The skyscrapers built during the period were designed along the lines of structures pioneered in America. Often they seemed tall enough to interfere with the heavens.

2 *"'Sall right, Bill—I've gotcha"* (Nicholls, *Bulletin*, 1936). Jokes about steeplejacks flourished in the early days of skyscrapers.

3 *"Maggie, where the devil are you?"* (Lang, *Smith's Weekly*, 1936). Early patrons of the 'talkies' were as unpopular if they themselves talked during the screening as they are today.

4 *"Turn the wireless up"* (Jolliffe, *Bulletin*, 1940). The magic of radio brings civilization to Saltbush Bill and the backblocks.

5 *"You're on the air in ten seconds"* (McGregor, *Bulletin*, 1946). Early radio performers were renowned for filling the silences with 'ers' and 'ahs', and it was some time before the art of speaking live on air was perfected.

1

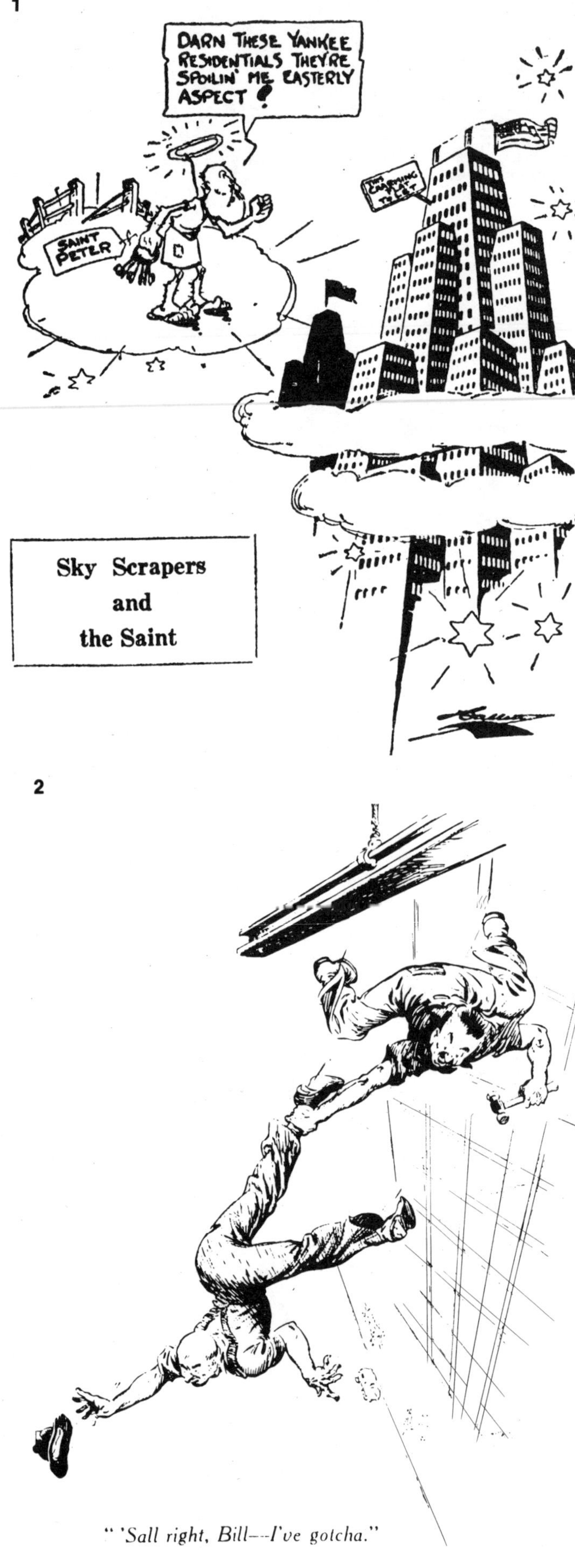

2

" 'Sall right, Bill—I've gotcha."

"Maggie, where the devil are you?"

4

"Turn the wireless up so I kin 'ear it goin' round me traps, Mo."

5

"You're on the air in ten seconds, and remember—no 'ers,' 'ahs' or 'ahems'!"

1927–1936
Fancy Fashions: What Next?

The many and varied fashions of the interwar period all reflected the desire to be light-hearted. The styles of the early 1920s broke away from the formality of Edwardian and Victorian traditions. Women's dresses became narrow tubes in which the breasts vanished and the waist either slipped down to the hips or disappeared altogether. The figures that preoccupied earlier generations were abandoned, and as the roaring twenties hotted up, the hems rose to reveal the dancing legs of the good-time girls. By the 1930s short skirts were exposing knees and raising eyebrows. A turning point was reached, however, and as the clouds of war gathered again skirts returned to an appropriately sober length, where they remained until the permissive 1960s.

1 *Some Time Long Ago* (Gall, *Bulletin*, 1927). Garments of the day flap in the breezy atmosphere of nonchalance that characterized the 1920s.

2 *Flapper friend* (Hallett, *Smith's Weekly*, 1928). Two good-time girls of the period doll up for a dance.

3 *"Don't talk so loud, dear"* (Virgil, *Smith's Weekly*, 1927). After exposing the knee in the late 1920s the rising hem froze for some years before slipping back down to a position more commensurate with the troubled 1930s.

4 *Rector: Isn't it terrible?* (Virgil, *Smith's Weekly*, 1936). The Church fought a losing battle as more of the female body was exposed in public places.

5 *The man with the hammer* (Jonsson, *Smith's Weekly*, 1927). The effects of the rising hemline were often dramatic.

1

SOME TIME LONG AGO.
SHE (*brightly*): "I'm afraid I've kept you waiting. When did you get here?"
HE (*bitterly*): "I forget the exact date."

2

Flapper friend: Did your new boss shake hands when you met him?
Typiste: No, he just said "How do you do?" and kissed me.

3

"Don't talk so loud, dear; you're attracting attention."

4

Rector: Isn't it terrible the way these girls loll about the beaches with hardly anything on?
Curate: Yes, I'd like to see them in church.

5

The man with the hammer: Ain't she a stunner!

CHAPTER VII

Behind the Brisbane Line 1939–1946

Back to War
Too Little Too Late
Women at War
The Austerity Campaign
Digging In
Japs in the Chookhouse
All's Fair in Love and War
They Did Their Bit
Fancy Fashions: What Next?

CHAPTER VII
Behind the Brisbane Line 1939–1946

A date with Hitler

The advent of World War II effectively ended the internal disagreements that had troubled Australia during the previous decade. Whereas the Great War had divided the country over the issue of conscription for overseas service, World War II united citizens around a common cause. Enlistment rose sharply after the Japanese bombed Pearl Harbour in 1941, and all differences were buried as the nation met its first attack on home ground when Darwin was attacked in 1942. Vows to defend the homeland to the last person and the last shilling were the catch-cries of the day. Even though it had opposed participation in the Great War, the *Australian Worker* now declared, 'It is not in the Australian make-up to squib a fight, no matter how hard and bitter the conflict may be'. And so cartoonists were guaranteed a popular subject, and one that was to provide them with material for six long years.

Australians formed themselves into a National Emergency Service of 300 000 male and female volunteers who were trained in first aid, fire-fighting and aircraft spotting. A corps of defence wardens was created to supervise activities during air raids and to provide instructions on the building of air raid shelters and the wearing of gas masks. 'Blackouts' and 'brownouts' were introduced, buildings had to be barricaded, street names and signs removed to confuse any invading forces and constant air raid drill provided for civilians and school children.

By the end of the war, more than one million people out of a population of seven million were serving the war effort in some capacity. Many women enlisted, serving at home or abroad, while others sprang into the vacancies left by men in the essential industries. They formed the basis of the 3 000 strong Land Army to maintain the supply of fresh fruit and vegetables; others provided accommodation for the 4 600 American troops who arrived in 1941 to defend Australia.

With everyone tightening their belts in response to the austerity campaign, class lines were blurred and people of different socio-economic origins queued together for sugar and other luxuries. The wealthy were discouraged from employing servants, and elaborate clothing was frowned upon when standard garments—sometimes made from sugar and rice bags —were issued and women's dress became plain and functional. Since everybody was restricted to rations, people experimented with substitutes in an attempt to overcome the shortages. A spirit of egalitarianism pervaded the community, a united cause making it easier to bear the deprivations. Everyone was employed and working for the good of the country.

These were the themes that interested the cartoonists who in turn did their bit by boosting morale during the war. They called upon the populace to defend the barricades long before the Japanese struck; some of them had predicted the second war as far back as 1916, and now called upon the government to bring the troops back home to defend their own country. They saw the need for American rather than British military support and cheered as the Americans arrived, little realizing the significance of this cultural turning point in Australian social history.

The daily papers, adding their voices to *Smith's Weekly* and the *Bulletin*, gave the nation more outlets for cartoonists than it had ever had before. Rousing propaganda poured from the presses to support the war effort and to inspire even greater sacrifices. Mick Armstrong of the Melbourne *Argus* emerged during the period to challenge the older artists on the weeklies and set the scene for the age of the daily newspaper cartoonists.

The identity of Australia at this time was the mature digger, less cocky than before and undoubtedly more professional. He was not one to rush into the fray, but when there he would fight with all the courage of his father, the Anzac. There were, of course, some who were reluctant to see Australia involved, but when the country was attacked the defender rose up straight and strong; Australians stood together, united *Behind The Brisbane Line*.

Willing but not able

1939–1940
Back to War

The outbreak of World War II was not greeted with the same enthusiasm as that of the Great War. The enormous losses of the first war had left a deep scar on the Australian memory and there was a far greater reluctance to become involved. Certainly a respectable number had volunteered for the Australian Imperial Force and a contingent of 20 000 sailed for the front early in 1940. In place of the emotional appeals in the posters of the Great War, the recruiting campaigns of World War II remained fairly low key until Australia itself was directly threatened.

1 *Cradle Song* (Low, *Bulletin*, 1916). A defeated Hun waiting for his son to grow up so that Germany may be avenged is portrayed here in a prophetic cartoon drawn twenty years before Germany repudiated the Versailles Treaty and took the Rhineland.

Cradle Song

Hushabye, baby, grow sturdy and strong:
Hushabye, babchen, der var vill be long:
If you vas older, mein Faderland's son.
Ve teach you der Kultur, ve gif you a gun.
Ven lusty young Shermans to manhood arrive
Dey die dat der Kaiser may still keep alive.
Unless in der meantime der Nation gets sense
You'll make cannon-fodder some twenty years hence.

2 *"Don't want no cavalry, eh?"* (Scorfield, *Bulletin*, 1940). The technological advances between the wars were to transform the character of international conflict.

3 *"Fancy the old cow remembering"* (*Bulletin*, 1940). Since the conflicts were only twenty years apart many returned to the front line to pick up where they had left off.

4 *Bluey: I'll shoot the next flamin' Tommy* (Dunne, *Smith's Weekly*, 1939). Like his father, the son of the Anzac was called a 'digger' throughout World War II.

1

2

"Don't want no cavalry, eh? All right, then. Gee-up, Flash!"

3

"Fancy the old cow remembering where he put 'em after all these years!"

4

BLUEY: I'll shoot the next flamin' Tommy who asks why they call us "Diggers."

1939–1941
Too Little Too Late

Because of the belief, shared with the Allies, that the fascists could be dissuaded from war, Australia was unprepared for the conflict. The constant cry of the military enthusiasts was that reinforcements and supplies were always 'too little too late'. Military equipment had been allowed to run down between the wars and the air force, navy and army were all embarrassingly short. There were only 2 800 in the Australian Army at the start of the war. Enlistment in the three services grew from 3 000 to 993 000 by the conclusion of the war. Many soldiers were untrained and so the cartoonists had a heyday responding to their early efforts.

1 *Mr. Menzies' Perfect Soldier* (Mahoney, *Daily News*, 1939). Low pay and inadequate clothing hampered early recruitment and created pressure for a greater defence budget. It was Prime Minister Menzies who announced Australia's war with Germany on 3 September.

2 *"Have it your own way"* (Rice, *Bulletin*, 1940). Although Australians distinguished themselves in the air there were many teething troubles.

3 *"Any Complaints?"* (Cousin, *Bulletin*, 1941). The traditional jokes about Army mess food were as popular as ever.

4 *"Dinkum, boys"* (Jolliffe, *Bulletin*, 1940). Saltbush Bill advises the army as they set up defences to protect Australia.

5 *"You haven't quite got the idea"* (Listed, *Bulletin*, 1939). Aborigines, who enlisted in greater numbers in World War II than they had in the Great War, brought their own special skills to the conflict.

1

MR. MENZIES' PERFECT SOLDIER

2

"Have it your own way. I still think we're flying too low!"

3

"Any complaints?"

4

"*Dinkum, boys, that's the lousiest line o' fencin' I ever seen.*"

5

"*You haven't quite got the idea, Private Quartpot.*"

1940–1944
Women at War

Women played a major role in World War II, serving outside Australia as well as running the country at home. More than 52 000 women were in the women's services abroad and thousands worked for the National Emergency Service, the Land Army, the Red Cross, in munitions factories and in essential services, including the departments administering the National Security Regulations, which regulated prices, labour, production, resources and the rationing of food and clothing. Despite their crucial role they became, as always, a favourite topic for cartoonists.

1 *"Yes, gents?"* (Such, *Bulletin*, 1942). The female invasion of the sacred male temple caused a few raised eyebrows during the war.

2 *"All right, girls"* (Donald, *Bulletin*, 1941). Despite jokes about their sensitivity Australian women proved as tough as the men when tested.

3 *"We're almost doubling our output, sister"* (White, *Bulletin*, 1941). The government called upon the people to double their output to help win the war.

4 *"I don't think I could ever go back"* (Lindsay, *Bulletin*, 1944). Misrepresentation aside, women served in almost every capacity during the war.

5 *"He wants his arm set"* (Jolliffe, *Bulletin*, 1940). Jokes about bandaging abounded during the conflict.

6 *"I said your rip cord"* (Such, *Bulletin*, 1941). In truth, women played a vital part in the operations of the air force.

1

"Yes, gents?"

2

"All right, girls. You're **NOT** *a lot of nincompoops!"*

3

"We're almost doubling our output, sister."

4

"I don't think I could ever go back to housework after this!"

5

"He wants his arm set in some OTHER position, doctor."

6

"I said your rip cord—not your zipper!"

1940–1944
The Austerity Campaign

The National Security Regulations established during the war enabled the government to impose censorship and control prices, resources, production and labour. Commodities, clothing and food were rationed when in short supply and people were issued with a ration book of tear-out coupons which they exchanged for scarce goods such as petrol, coal, meat, tea, cigarettes, sugar and a wide range of 'non-essential' goods including double-breasted suits, waistcoats, footwear, toys, confectionery and alcohol. The shortages inspired an austerity campaign in which everybody was urged to share, find substitutes or do without.

1 *The Once-Welcome Stranger* (Lindsay, *Bulletin*, 1944). The arrival of a baby, once a joyful occasion, only meant increased hardships for many during the difficult war years.

2 *"We girls know"* (*Bulletin*, 1942). Charcoal fuel stored in a bag on the roof produced gas which powered cars during the petrol shortage.

3 *"Got any firewood?"* (McGregor, *Bulletin*, 1941). Coal shortages during the war were caused by a lack of labour in the mines.

4 *"That's near enough"* (Scorfield, *Bulletin*, 1941). The shortage of building materials resulted in many improvizations.

5 *"Gentlemen"* (*Bulletin*, 1942). Apart from sharing the limited supply of tobacco, smokers tried musk leaves and gum leaves as substitutes.

1

THE ONCE-WELCOME STRANGER.

2

"We girls know when you men DO *run out of gas these days."*

"Got any firewood or old papers y' don't want, lady? We've run out o' coal."

4

"That's near enough—we can fill in the rest with putty!"

5

"Gentlemen, I regret to say that the Austerity smoking circle has exceeded its weekly quota by half an ounce."

1938–1942
Digging In

Only when the Japanese attacked Pearl Harbour did Australians really begin to fear invasion. With many of their forces abroad the largely undefended population began to take precautions. The National Emergency Services stepped up their training and recruitment; surface air-raid shelters were built in the larger cities; buildings were protected from blast by baffle walls and sandbags; householders were advised to dig trenches or construct covered shelters; tin helmets were issued; respirators were stored at the ready and the beaches were fortified with tank-traps, barbed wire, concrete pill boxes and gun emplacements. When Singapore fell in January 1942 invasion seemed only a matter of time.

1 *"This'll be one bit of information"* (Lindsay, *Bulletin*, 1942). Any signposts that might have guided an invading army were taken down, as were those of hotels that bore place names.

2 *"If we 'av t' fall back"* (Jolliffe, *Bulletin*, 1942). Explosives and inflammable material were stored by the last-ditch stand 'denial squad' at key points along the expected invasion route.

3 *"Not now, Ted"* (*Bulletin*, 1942). A top secret 'denial squad' was trained to destroy important industrial plants and strategic bridges ahead of the invading army.

4 *Too Fat To Fight Or Run* (Lindsay, *Bulletin*, 1939). With a population of one and a quarter million Sydney was considered a 'deathtrap' by those who feared air attack.

5 *Solemn League and Covenant* (Lindsay, *Bulletin*, 1938). The natives preparing to meet the Japanese.

6 *"Stop, George"* (*Bulletin*, 1942). Although people were advised to build their own air-raid shelters, many were of dubious value.

7 *"An' I say it CAN happen here"* (White, *Bulletin*, 1942). Air raid drill was held in factories, offices and schools and many devised their own personal form of shelter.

1

"This'll be one bit of information the Japs won't get!"

2

"If we 'ave t' fall back, we're doin' what the Russians did—blow the dam up."

3

"Not now, Ted. Wait till they get 'alfway across."

4

TOO FAT TO FIGHT OR RUN.

5

SOLEMN LEAGUE AND COVENANT FOR SELF-PRESERVATION.

6

"Stop, George, I think I will have the trench over in the corner after all."

7

"An' I say it CAN *happen here."*

1939–1943 Japs in the Chookhouse

When the Japanese eventually attacked Australia, they bombed Darwin and nine other towns in the north, shelled Sydney and Newcastle and sent midget submarines into Port Jackson where they sank a ferry that was used as a naval depot. At least 238 people were killed in the early raids on Darwin and 19 naval ratings died when the ferry sank. Although Darwin was bombed 58 more times and homes in Rose Bay, Bellevue Hill and Bondi were damaged, no other lives were lost. The arrival of American forces and their victory in the battle of Midway spelt the end of the threat from Japan.

1 *Long Ear Of Coincidence* (Mahoney, *Daily Telegraph*, 1942). People were warned not to say things in public that may have been overheard by spies and transmitted to the Japanese.

2 *"There's something wrong with that bloke, Joe!"* (*Bulletin*, 1942). Although the Japanese land army never invaded, 378 prisoners of war escaped from a prisoner-of-war camp in Cowra, New South Wales, and roamed the roads for nine days before being recaptured.

3 *Long-Distance Thinking* (Mahoney, *Daily Telegraph*, 1942). British war-time Prime Minister Churchill used the telephone which had linked the two countries since 1930 to assure Australian Prime Minister Curtin that Japan would not invade.

4 *Japscotch* (Lindsay, *Bulletin*, 1943). With American help the Australians drove the Japanese back from their doorstep.

1

LONG EAR OF COINCIDENCE

2

"There's something wrong with that bloke, Joe!"

LONG-DISTANCE THINKING

4

JAPSCOTCH.

1940–1944 All's Fair in Love and War

Cupid did a roaring trade upon the announcement of World War II. As many men secured the girl of their choice before leaving for the front, the number of marriages rose markedly. But marrying a soldier bound for the front was not as likely to result in widowhood in World War II as it had been in the Great War. Whereas 60 000 Australians died in World War I less than 30 000 died in World War II. Cartoonists consequently had a feast as they showed their countrymen and women a lighter side of the conflict.

1 *This "phony war!"* (*Bulletin*, 1940). The lull which followed Britain's declaration of war on Germany enabled Australian soldiers to put their affairs in order.

2 *"Greater love hath no man"* (Morris, *Bulletin*, 1942). Tobacco became very scarce during the war.

3 *"Money, my foot!"* (Frith, *Bulletin*, 1942). Ration books were highly prized during the war.

4 *"Does a lady called Daisy"* (McGregor, *Bulletin*, 1940). A fanciful war-time caller.

5 *"We used to keep our pants up"* (Scorfield, *Bulletin*, 1944). Legends similar to those of the Anzacs were generated by the action of World War II.

6 *"An important announcement"* (Lock, *Bulletin*, 1941). Rivalry between the forces was strong in both love and war.

1

This "phony war"!

2

"Greater love hath no man than this. . . . !"

3

"Money, my foot! She's marrying him for his tea ration."

4

"Does a lady called Daisy live here?"

5

"We used to keep our pants up with those in New Guinea."

6

"An important announcement, list'ners! All officers and men from the squadron are to report on board their ships immediately!"

1940–1946
They Did Their Bit

At home, there were many who either were opposed in principle to the war or used the conflict to make their fortunes. There were nearly 3 000 conscientious objectors who resisted conscription when it was introduced. Others preferred to get on with their favourite pastimes of drinking or surfing rather than support the war effort. The black market which came into operation following the government restrictions brought fortunes to the profiteers who dealt in drink, fruit, clothing, toys and any other rationed foodstuffs and commodities. When the war ended, however, these differences were buried as the nation turned to meet its next challenge.

1 *Black-Market Dialogue (Lindsay, Bulletin*, 1943). Businessmen trading in rationed foodstuffs made a fortune on the black market.

2 *Star Boarders* (Pidgeon, *Daily Telegraph*, 1942). Feeling ran strong among the troops who came home on leave to find others taking it easy.

3 *"Now, do you believe me?"* (*Bulletin*, 1944). Returning soldiers were often annoyed by the disinterest shown by those who had stayed at home.

4 *Family Dawn Service* (Lindsay, *Bulletin*, 1946). The Anzac of the Great War, his son, who defended Australia against the Japanese, and his grandson steel themselves to meet the future.

1

BLACK-MARKET DIALOGUE.

"But I can't pay those prices on my husband's service pay."
"Then get out and make room for those who can."

2

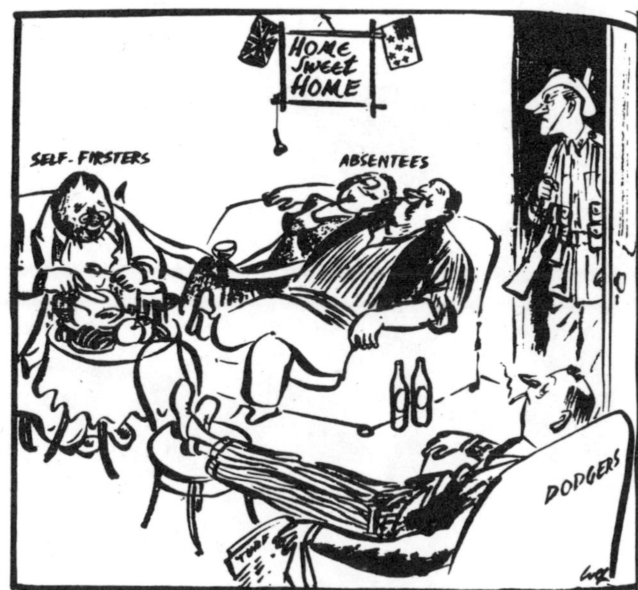

Star Boarders

3

"Now, do you believe me?"

4

FAMILY DAWN SERVICE.
"Whatever's coming, we'll take it together in the old spirit."

1937–1946
Fancy Fashions: What Next?

Government regulations influenced the fashions of the war period considerably. A National Council for Clothes Styling fixed the length for skirts at a respectable level and advised women to substitute leg paint for stockings. Dolman, balloon and leg-of-mutton sleeves were banned to save cloth; accessories, other than belts up to two inches wide, and petticoats, were prohibited; and the manufacture of evening frocks was suspended. The Austerity Campaign put an end to experimentation in fashion as women concentrated on contributing to the war effort. Perhaps it was these shortages that brought nudity on the beaches that little bit closer.

1 *Ours must be fully a week out of date* (Morrison, *Smith's Weekly*, 1937). Although it was the fashion to change outfits regularly up to the war, the conflict put an immediate end to such indulgences.

2 *"Would you move over to the left?"* (Lock, *Bulletin*, 1942). Gun emplacements along the shores took many by surprise, including those who dared to bathe nude on secret beaches.

3 *"It's things like 'er"* (Scorfield, *Bulletin*, 1944). War-time austerity encouraged women to wear trousers.

4 *"That doesn't apply to me"* (Lock, *Bulletin*, 1946). Due to the clothing shortage the government encouraged people to wear the same outfits for as long as possible.

5 *Beach-Fashions Of To-day* (Morrison, *Smith's Weekly*, 1937). The nude beaches of today are here predicted forty years before their time.

1

2

"Would you move over to the left, please—you're right in line with my telescope!"

3

"It's things like 'er wot tears the veil of mystery from us girls."

4

"That doesn't apply to me—every stitch I'm wearing is pre-war."

5

BEACH-FASHIONS OF TO-DAY will soon be just a sentimental joke . . .

CHAPTER VIII
Striking It Rich 1947–1967

Post-War Pinching
Getting It Easy
The New Australians
Crowning Glory
On the Silver Screen
On the World Stage
The Sydney Ocker House
The State Replaces God
Rocking the Establishment
Modern Miracles
Disaster Strikes
Fancy Fashions: What Next?

CHAPTER VIII
Striking It Rich
1947–1967

The lucky Australians

For those who had lived through the depression and remembered the wars, the boom years of the 1950s arrived like a hard-earned reward. Following immediately on the heels of the Austerity Campaign of World War II, the new-found wealth intoxicated Australians who could not believe their luck. Hardly had post-war rationing ended in 1950 when in 1951 the wool and mineral boom began to lift the economy onto a plateau that was sustained for the next twenty years.

Australians could hardly have lost during the 1950s, for whenever they turned over a sod of earth they found a gleaming mineral on the spade. Uranium was discovered in the Northern Territory at Rum Jungle in 1949 and in Queensland at Mary Kathleen in 1954. Oil was found at Exmouth Gulf in Western Australia in 1953, in the Moonie Fields in Queensland in 1961 and again along with gas in Bass Strait in 1965. Bauxite was found at Weipa in 1953 and at Gove in 1964.

Power was developed through the work of the Snowy Mountains Authority which generated its first electricity in 1955. Water resources were tapped with schemes such as the Ord River (1963) and the Warragamba and Keepit dams (1960). The Atomic Energy Commission, established in 1953, built a nuclear reactor at Lucas Heights, New South Wales, in 1958. Finance was available through the Commonwealth Development Bank formed in 1959. Trade was blossoming, with massive wheat sales to China and Russia. Apart from the temporary credit squeeze during 1961–2, it seemed that the country was locked into a one-way growth pattern that had an inevitable exponential destination.

During this period of rapid economic growth, Australia attracted thousands of migrants annually with its high wages, forty-hour week (from 1948) and a high standard of living. The millionth migrant arrived in 1955 and another million followed before the end of 1967 to bring the total population to eleven million. Visits by Queen Elizabeth II, the first by a reigning British monarch, and the first visit by an American president, L. B. Johnson, in 1966, focussed attention on Australia, as did the Olympic Games held in Melbourne in 1956.

The prevailing atmosphere of stability and conservatism riled the traditionally cheeky cartoonists who chided the conscience of the complacent masses and called out for a change. Their preoccupations included the bad treatment migrants received, the tight censorship laws, increasing violence and permissiveness and a host of blunders ranging from a subsiding Melbourne bridge to the bungling over the Sydney Opera House. Rapid social changes also gave the cartoonists an endless stream of subjects. The musical world was shaken alive by the rock 'n' roll era, which in turn gave way to the pop tunes perfected by the Beatles and then hard rock. Beer drinking was challenged by drug-taking. The first walk by humans on the moon made science fiction a reality.

The daily newspapers finally asserted themselves as leaders of the cartoon world; with modern techniques they were able to reproduce and generously display top quality work overnight. Early newspaper cartoonists included Sydney's George Finey, Bill Mahoney, Molnar, Eyre Jnr, Bruce Petty, Emile Mercier and Jolliffe; Melbourne's Frith, Jeff and Weg; Brisbane's Ian Gall; Adelaide's Pat Oliphant; and Perth's Paul Rigby.

The representative figure of Australia changed during this period and varied between cities. Generally, however, it was an optimistic upstanding middle-class gent in a sensible suit and broad-brimmed hat that stood for Australians. Melbourne's Australian was Frith's whiskered commuter, caught with his pants down, and Sydney's was the little family man, farewelling the Queen.

Thus was the spectacular recovery after the war applauded enthusiastically by cartoonists of the 1950s and 1960s. At last the formula for prosperity was complete: there were abundant resources, a plentiful labour supply and a steady source of capital. Exports were high, investment became common and there were jobs for all. The day of the Australians was at hand, a day that was to last twenty years up to the eve of their next major war, when things once again turned sour. But until that time, all of them were lucky Australians enjoying the undreamt-of experience of *Striking It Rich.*

Bushmen to the last

1949–1952
Post-War Pinching

The effects of the war-time Austerity Campaign lasted until 1951 when the petrol rationing was finally lifted. Meat and clothes rationing was lifted in 1948 but there were still shortages in the early 1950s. Foodstuffs such as butter, eggs and milk and commodities such as wool and wheat, were controlled in varying degrees by the government until 1952. Some were worried that the increasing population, and particularly the large numbers of migrants, would create a situation where there were too many mouths to feed. The economy began to take off, however, with the wool and mineral boom in 1951 guaranteeing enough for all.

1 *"A beautiful fit, sir!"* (Tanner, *Daily Telegraph*, 1952). Clothing restrictions lasted until 1952 despite the end of rationing in 1948.

2 *"Mind if I squeeze"* (Dixon, *Smith's Weekly*, 1949). Petrol rationing was not lifted until 1951.

3 *The Ghost Walks* (Heth, *Bulletin*, 1950). Inflation, that age-old spectre, appeared briefly on the horizon in the post-war period before the boom arrived to banish it for two decades.

4 *Taking It Seriously!* (Frith, *Sydney Morning Herald*, 1949). Despite their own shortages Australians sent food parcels to people in greater need in Britain.

5 *Everything But The Money* (Gall, *Courier Mail*, 1952). Many could not afford to build their own homes until the boom years of the mid-1950s began to release the finance.

1

"A beautiful fit, sir!"

2

"Mind if I squeeze the last drop out myself?"

3

THE GHOST WALKS.

4

TAKING IT SERIOUSLY!

The Minister for Commerce and Agriculture, Mr. Pollard, says that Australia's increasing population will force the importing of food unless primary production is increased.

British Housewife: "Oh dear, perhaps we should send it back to them!"

5

EVERTHING BUT THE MONEY

1953–1961
Getting It Easy

The relief that the good years brought Australians in the 1950s is apparent in the cartoons of the period. But although some show the sheer joy of a nation that had struck it rich at last, others reveal that there were many who just could not believe it, and still others who warned that it would not last. Discoveries of uranium, oil, natural gas and bauxite promised a bonanza for the country and it soon became clear that all their Christmases had come at once for the lucky Australians.

1 *"A pity you wasn't closer to the city"* (Mercier, *Sun*, 1960). Oil discoveries, a bountiful economy and the manufacture of 'Australia's own car' the Holden (1948), boosted motoring and the petrol industry during the period.

2 *"— and I promise"* (King, *Daily Telegraph*, 1961). Gigantic trade surpluses and a healthy domestic economy ensured the reigning Liberals unchallenged leadership for over two decades.

3 *"I hope this doesn't make him"* (King, *Daily Telegraph*, 1961). The discovery of oil in the Moonie Fields in Queensland in 1961 added to Australia's great wealth.

4 *"Getting It Easy"—But For How Long?* (Gall, *Courier Mail*, 1953). Despite the oil and uranium finds there were some with memories of the lean years who could not believe it would last.

5 *The Brighter Side* (Gall, *Courier Mail*, 1956). The wool boom which took off in 1951, when the record price of £1 was paid for one pound of wool, precipitated the economic growth of the period.

1

"A pity you wasn't closer to the city. The petrol companies'd pay a fortune for a corner block like this!"

2

"— and I promise prosperity'll be just around the corn—ouch!"

3

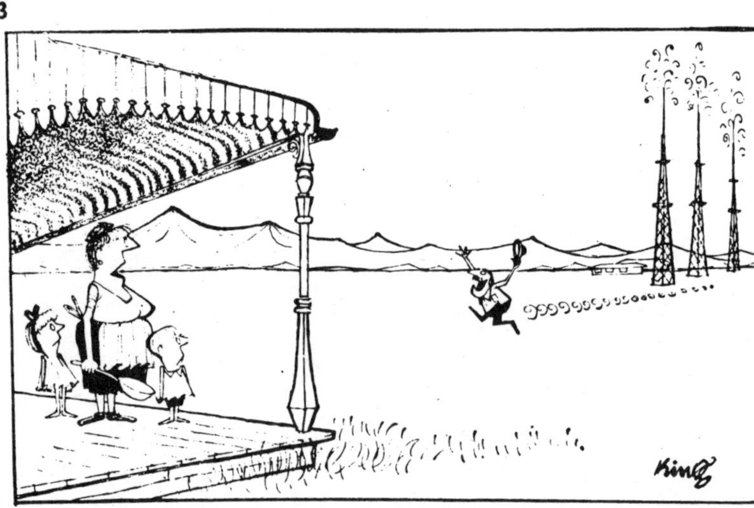

"I hope this doesn't make him like those Arab oil sheiks with stables of Cadillacs and dancing girls."

4

"GETTING IT EASY"—BUT FOR HOW LONG? ———— by Ian Gall

5

WOO£ RISE

BRISBANE SALES

GLOOM

AUST.

MIDDLE-EAST SETBACKS

THE BRIGHTER SIDE ———————— by Ian Gall

1952–1968
The New Australians

The post-war immigration programme began in 1947 when the first 'displaced persons' arrived in Australia. The government, concerned both that the low population would tempt a would-be invader, and also conscious of the need for labour, began to solicit Europeans who had lost homes or jobs during the war. One million arrived to supplement the eight million strong nation within the first eight years of the programme, and a second million came by the end of 1967. With a traditionally Anglo-Saxon background Australians did not prove to be the best of hosts and often failed to provide the facilities needed for such a massive influx of people.

1 *Unemployment Rock* (Frith, Melbourne *Herald*, 1952). Before the newly discovered resources stimulated the boom, many migrants in the early 1950s found it difficult to get a job.

2 *The New Australian* (Scorfield, *Bulletin*, 1956). Although the spectre of automation worried many, it was the new Australian who actually did much of the dreary and back-breaking work to develop the resources in the post-war economy.

3 *"Cheer up everyone!"* (Rigby, Adelaide *Advertiser*, 1963). The facilities provided through the 'assisted passage' scheme were not always adequate and some migrants were left to find their own way to Australia.

4 *"They're spending more money on migrant hostels"* (Tanner, *Age*, 1968). The Nissen huts and compounds used to house migrants during the great influx were criticized by many.

5 *Untrained* (Oliphant, Adelaide *Advertiser*, 1962). Transport facilities for the new arrivals were often below those expected of a host country destined to benefit from the increased labour force afforded by the migrants.

1

2

THE NEW AUSTRALIAN

3

"Cheer up everyone! We'll soon be in South Africa, or Canada, or SOMEWHERE . . ."

4

'They're spending more money on migrant hostels — has the price of barbed wire gone up?'

5

"I'm sorry, madam. This is reserved for people."

1953–1954
Crowning Glory

The dark cloud that hung over patriotic Australians following the death of King George VI in 1952 was blown away by the coronation of the young Queen Elizabeth II in 1953. Her sunny disposition and optimism warmed the hearts of Australians who celebrated the royal event in every corner of the country. If this demonstration of Empire loyalty, which coincided with the conquest of Mt Everest, was not sufficient, then the reception she received when she toured the country in 1954 would have established the colonial faith in the monarchy as never before. Members of the Royal Family had earlier toured the country but this was the first time a *reigning* monarch had landed in Australia.

1 *£100,000,000 SPREE* (Low, *Guardian*, 1953). The London cartoon by New Zealander David Low was one of the few voices raised in protest over the coronation and he was severely reprimanded by British authorities and the public.

2 *"She's Passing Now!"* (Gall, *Courier Mail*, 1954). The crowds that lined the streets during the Queen's tour of Australia demonstrated the enthusiasm for the monarchy.

3 *Modern Version* (Eyre Jnr, *Sydney Morning Herald*, 1954). The Queen is welcomed to Australia with a respect once demonstrated by Sir Walter Raleigh to an earlier queen of the same name.

4 *Everest* (Frith, Melbourne *Herald*, 1954). As if by plan, the world's last unclimbed peak was conquered by Empire subjects Edmund Hillary (New Zealand) and Norgay Tensing (Nepal) on the eve of the coronation.

5 *On The Crest* (Gall, *Courier Mail*, 1954). The loyalty demonstrated over the coronation of the Queen indicated the Empire had never been stronger.

6 *Her Land* (Gall, *Courier Mail*, 1954). Queensland comes into its own.

1

2

"SHE'S PASSING NOW!" by Ian Gall

3

MODERN VERSION

4

5

ON THE CREST ——— by Ian Gall

6

HER LAND ——— by Ian Gall

1946–1949
On the Silver Screen

Cartoons about the impending arrival of television began appearing in the late 1940s. The British had been experimenting with TV from 1926 but it was not until after World War II that transmission was successfully established in Europe and the United States. Although Australians had been experimenting with such devices as the 1929 Miles mechanical scanning broadcast system in Melbourne, and the Brisbane cathode ray tube transmission demonstrations by Tom Elliott in 1935, the country had to wait until the EMI system was perfected and imported from Europe. This happened just in time for the 1956 Olympic Games.

1 *"Now, then"* (Heth, *Bulletin*, 1946). One of the first cartoons on the introduction of television raises a common problem.

2 *"Ah! Jolly good play"* (*Smith's Weekly*, 1949). Imagined highlights of future broadcasts.

3 *"Struth!"* (Smith, *Smith's Weekly*, 1949). Televised parliament was expected with the arrival of television.

4 *Hell-Evision* (*Smith's Weekly*, 1949). The disadvantages of the new gadget were well anticipated by the cartoonists of the pre-television age.

1

"Now, then, that isn't in the book."

2

"Ah! Jolly good play, Bedser, old man, jolly good play!"

3

HELL-EVISION

This television is not all it's cracked up to be. It has more disadvantages than most people imagine, as Smith's artists can show. One thing, you can't walk around the house and listen, like you can with radio—you have to watch the confounded thing. And what happens . . . .

• THE housework is bound to suffer!

• AND it's not everybody who will want to be in the dark.

• THEN the children will have to be locked out for some programmes.

• AND what about its effect on some of the poor radio players?

• MEDICAL science, too, will have another problem to solve.

• AND it's sure to embarrass some people at first!

• THEN the distracted S.P. punter will have something more to annoy him.

• AND what about when they take it to night clubs?

• FINALLY, if you have a television set, your home will become like a theatre.

1953–1956
On the World Stage

When the Duke of Edinburgh opened the Olympic Games in Melbourne in November 1956, the international sporting spotlight swung towards Australia. Australian athletes had performed well in earlier Olympics but on their home ground they distinguished themselves, gaining a record 13 gold medals. In swimming they won all the freestyle events, the relay and individual and they won all three places in men's and women's 100 metres. With champions such as Dawn Fraser and Lorraine Crapp—who broke 18 world records in training—Australia emerged as the greatest nation of swimmers in the world.

1 *Now, Don't Let It Go Out* (Gall, *Courier Mail*, 1953). There were fears that Melbourne would not be ready in time for the games, as the International Olympic Council had only confirmed the venue three years before.

2 *"Siesta at the Mechanics Institute"* (Armstrong, *Argus*, 1954). Strikes and bungling delayed the completion of the overall plan of assembly for the Melbourne Olympic Games complex.

3 *"57 varieties"* (Armstrong, *Argus*, 1956). Showers threatened to disrupt the games when Melbourne's proverbial rain set in just before the opening.

4 *"Hey! D'you want to start a bushfire?"* (Scorfield, *Bulletin*, 1956). The torch completed its last lap from Athens carried by a series of cross-country runners.

5 *A Time For Celebration* (Lindsay, *Bulletin*, 1956). The spirit of the games is caught in one of the last cartoons by the veteran artist in his fiftieth working year.

6 *Where there's a will . . .!* (Frith, Melbourne *Herald*, 1956). Capacity crowds packed the Melbourne Cricket Ground and other sports arenas during the events.

7 *"I'm sorry"* (Weg, Melbourne *Herald*, 1956). Despite the jokes the officials received international acclaim for their impartial and efficient administration of the games.

1

NOW, DON'T LET IT GO OUT THIS TIME !

2

"Siesta at the Mechanics Institute"

3

"57 varieties"

4

"Hey! D'you want to start a bushfire?"

5

A TIME FOR CELEBRATION!

6

Where there's a will . . .!

7

1960–1971
The Sydney Ocker House

The plans for an Opera House to be built on Benelong Point in Sydney's Port Jackson had been under way for some time when the lottery was begun in 1957 to finance the scheme. A contest held to solicit designs from architects and the public was won by the Danish architect, Joern Utzon, who then agreed to help make his concept a reality. Many problems were encountered during the construction of the Opera House and new designs forced upon Utzon in 1967 caused him to resign his position. The task was eventually completed, however, and the Opera House was opened by Queen Elizabeth II in 1973. It had taken many more years to build than anticipated and had cost not $7 million, as anticipated, but more than $100 million. But like the Sydney Harbour Bridge it had entertained a generation of cartoonists before the first ticket had even been sold.

1 *"What we should worry about"* (Mercier, *Sun*, 1960). Because the Opera House was taking so long to build many onlookers were grateful for its futuristic design.

2 *". . . And you have a go at the main foyer!"* (Petty, *Australian*, 1967). Australians were forced to fall back on their own skills when the Danish designer Joern Utzon resigned over forced changes in his plan.

3 *"Benelong junior there"* (Benier, *Daily Mirror*, 1971). Although the Aboriginal Land Rights issue began to emerge just as the Opera House was being completed, it was the rural areas that Aborigines wished to reclaim most of all.

4 *Sydney Soap Opera* (Petty, *Australian*, 1967). The rivalry between the Australian Broadcasting Commission and the Elizabethan Theatre Trust hampered much of the planning following the departure of Utzon.

5 *"Well, it's the best idea to date!"* (Petty, *Australian*, 1967). Because the Opera House had been built from the outside in as a concession to appearances, the acoustics became a problem due to an inferior auditorium that was designed late in the piece.

1

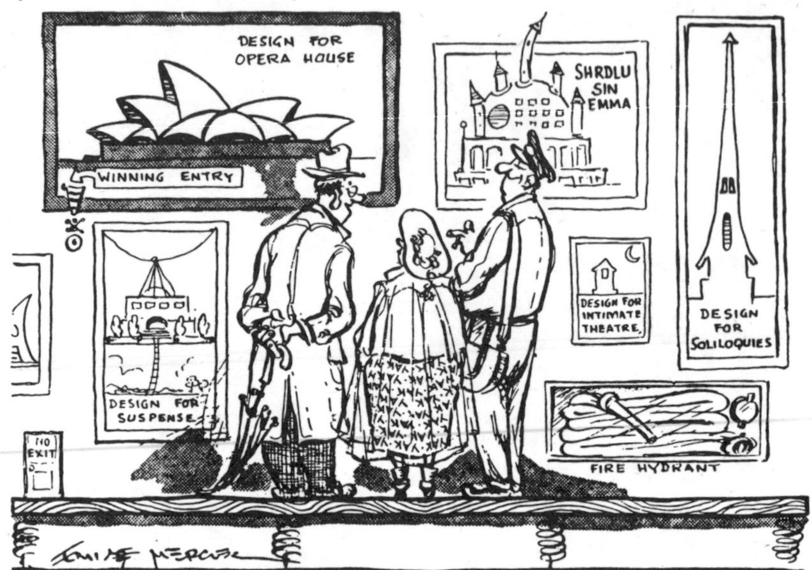

"What we should worry about is not so much the futuristic design as the fear of it being outmoded by the time they get it built!"

2

. . . and you have a go at the main foyer!'

3

"Benelong junior there — reckons we built it on an old tribal aluminium mine . . ."

4

SYDNEY SOAP OPERA

A funny thing happened on the way to the Opera House

5

'Well, it's the best idea to date!'

1952–1967
The State Replaces God

Some cartoonists saw the government as filling the vacuum created by the declining influence of the Church in the early 1960s. The State was beginning to tell people what they could and could not do or read. 'Thou shalt not . . .' edicts issued not from the pulpit but from the Minister's press secretary. It was also an age of rapidly changing social values when permissive behaviour evoked, or even provoked, reactionary and repressive social controls. The Church may have been more needed than ever before but its message seemed irrelevant, and so the State attempted to check the rising tide of misbehaviour, mainly through censorship.

1 *Sunday Observances Act* (Frith, Melbourne *Herald*, 1952). The Church was unable to persuade people to attend the congregations began dwindling during the period as the easily attained wealth bred a more secular community.

2 *"There can be no room within our Church"* (Sharp, *Australian*, 1965). Many felt that the Church was itself to blame for the decline in religion as its message was out of date.

3 *Shadows Of Shame* (Gall, *Courier Mail*, 1966). The increase in violence in the 1960s provoked some States to reintroduce capital punishment.

4 *"I don't care who you are"* (Tanner, *Bulletin*, 1964). With little training in artistic appreciation the police were sometimes guilty of banning classic works of art.

5 *"Banned any good books lately?"* (Petty, *Daily Mirror*, 1964). Many critics doubted the authority of those responsible for censorship in the early 1960s, claiming that books were banned simply because they contained references to sex.

1

2

"There can be no room within our Church for wretched, narrow-minded, out-of-date partisanship." *The Archbishop of Canterbury.*

3

SHADOWS OF SHAME

4

"I don't care who you are—get off the beach, you're improperly dressed."

5

"Banned any good books lately?"

1950–1966 Rocking the Establishment

Music changed greatly during the period with rock 'n' roll bursting onto the stage in the early 1950s and setting Australians—both young and old—jumping around to a totally new beat. Not since the 1920s had people danced in such a wild and abandoned manner. The generation let their hair down—literally. It was as if the release inspired by bands such as America's Bill Haley and the Comets and Australia's Johnny O'Keefe had been designed to allow those down under to celebrate the joys of their long-awaited prosperity. It was not to be long, however, before rock 'n' roll was to give way to another sort of sound—that of the Beatles.

1 *"See yer later, Alligater"* (Armstrong, *Argus*, 1952). The rock 'n' roll revolution of the early 1950s infected Australians of all ages.

2 *"I like these more sedate numbers"* (Jonsson, *Smith's Weekly*, 1950). Rock 'n' roll was difficult to define as a dance and enjoyed the same free movements that were characteristic of dances in the roaring twenties.

3 *"Really, Eve!"* (Eyre Jnr, *Sydney Morning Herald*, 1961). The new permissiveness brought a further change in moral standards and precipitated such scandals as that involving academics who were alleged to be exponents and practitioners of 'free love'.

4 *"Har! Har!"* (Rigby, *Daily Mirror*, 1964). The tour of Australia by the Beatles created record crowds and mass attacks of 'Beatlemania'.

5 *"John's taking me to a discotheque"* (Mercier, *Sun–Herald*, 1966). The new musical age created its own temple, the discotheque—where suitably clad 'rockers' off-loaded surplus energy.

1

2

"I like these more sedate numbers, don't you?"

3

"Really, Eve! Must you offer me a bite of that confounded thing at a time like this?"

4

"Har! Har!! Now YOU take your pick, Muldoon—the contingent for Cyprus or Operation Beatle-Crush . . . !"

5

'John's taking me to a discotheque—we'll be back in a couple of shakes.'

1956–1965
Modern Miracles

Technological progress was spectacular during the period, with the world moving from the air age into the space age. The first satellite—Sputnik I—was launched in 1957 by the Russians, and intercontinental missiles and nuclear bombs were developed to a terrifying degree of perfection. Australia, working in conjunction with the British and Americans, developed rocket and missile launching sites at Woomera in South Australia. The first satellite was launched from Woomera in 1967, six years after regular satellite tracking operations were initiated in Australia. Another development, the contraceptive pill, became widely used at this time, and changed the course of many women's lives.

1 *"This is the ultimate missile"* (Mercier, *Sun*, 1960). The guided missile entered the human arsenal, with Australia playing its part by offering communication facilities for American systems.

2 *"Of course the qualified economist"* (King, *Daily Telegraph*, 1963). Before decimal currency was introduced in 1966 there were competitions to find the best name for the different denominations.

3 *"Now that parking meters are in operation"* (Mercier, *Sun–Herald*, 1956). Parking meters were introduced to Sydney and then other cities in 1956.

4 *Pill Hits Birth Rate* (Bateup, *Bulletin*, 1965). The increasing use of the pill in the 1960s halted the birth rate.

5 *The Unwise Men Of The East* (Scorfield, *Bulletin*, 1957). The Russian satellite—Sputnik I—which ushered in the space age also alarmed those who feared communism.

1

"This is the ultimate missile to end all wars—it travels round the world right back to where it started from!"

2

"Of course the qualified economist will also require a degree in zoology

3

"Now that parking meters are in operation, get ready for the corny gag about someone cracking the jackpot!"

4

YEAH . . . WITH NO THANKS TO YOU

5

THE UNWISE MEN OF THE EAST

1954–1967
Disaster Strikes

After so many good years it seemed inevitable that the balloon would burst and Australia would be faced with bad times. By 1967 a turning point had been reached as the economy slowed down following bad seasons and the withdrawal of capital investment by both America and Britain. Inflation gathered momentum; industrial strikes began to dislocate the economy; pollution became a menace; Tasmania experienced disastrous bushfires and finally the Prime Minister, Harold Holt, drowned near Portsea, Victoria, and plunged the nation into an unhappy period of Christmas mourning. The fortunate 1950s and successful 1960s were over. There could be no going back; the boom years were already a memory.

1 *"If potatoes keep on soaring"* (Mercier, *Sun–Herald*, 1961). The credit squeeze of the early 1960s gave people a taste of the economic problems that were to follow.

2 *Drought Area* (Petty, *Australian*, 1965). Foreign investors began to bypass Australia as economic conditions became less favourable following bad seasons and industrial unrest.

3 *"File it away under sporting records"* (Molnar, *Sydney Morning Herald*, 1963). Industrial unrest—an unknown problem since World War II—began to trouble Australia as the 1960s progressed.

4 *"For years we've been leaving it off the map"* (Jeff, Melbourne *Herald*, 1967). The Tasmanian fires claimed 51 lives and caused $20 million damage in Hobart and southern Tasmania, burning down the Cascade Brewery into the bargain.

5 *Soot Menace* (Gall, *Courier Mail*, 1954). Cartoons attacking modern pollution began appearing in the mid-1950s.

6 *The Cruel Sea* (Atchison, Adelaide *Advertiser*, 1967). The disappearance of Australian Prime Minister, Harold Holt, while swimming off Portsea, seemed to spell the end of an era.

1

"If potatoes keep on soaring like that, we'll soon be able to call them spudniks!"

2

3

"File it away under sporting records."

4

"For years we've been leaving it off the map — let's help put it back . . . !"

5

6

1949–1966
Fancy Fashions: What Next?

The wealthy boom years did wonders for fashion in Australia. After the war women regained the flair they had celebrated during earlier periods such as the roaring twenties. This time, however, it was the 'new look' with wider, fuller skirts and nipped-in waistlines. Hemlines began to lower, pausing 18 centimetres above the bitumen. Some regarded the rebirth of 'high fashion' as regressive and compared it to pre-World War I styles. But fashions soon moved on, passing through a series of crazes including teddy boys, beatniks, rock 'n' roll and Beatlemania. Rough denim jeans began to clothe the young of both sexes and hemlines—as if to compete for attention—rose right up to create the outrageous mini-skirt.

1 *"They'll never get me into that silly fashion"* (Cullens, *Smith's Weekly*, 1949). The 'high fashion' fad which followed wartime restrictions attempted in vain to turn the clock back.

2 *"I'll toss you"* (Smith, *Smith's Weekly*, 1949). By the early 1950s the bikini was being pioneered on Sydney beaches.

3 *The Reason Why* (Oliphant, Adelaide *Advertiser*, 1963). Stiletto heels became a fad for some years during the early 1960s.

4 *On The Map* (Oliphant, Adelaide *Advertiser*, 1963). Tanya Verstak put Australia on the map when she won the title of Miss World.

5 *"Will it shrink?"* (Mercier, *Sun–Herald*, 1956). The same old question was posed for members of this generation as for those before them. Even if the material did not shrink it seemed inevitable as the 1960s approached that the ever-contracting bathing costume would disappear altogether.

1

"They'll never get ME into that silly fashion—it's taken me years to train the figure I've got!"

2

"I'll toss you who orders her off the beach!"

3

"Mind that cable with those sharp heels, Doris."

4

ON THE MAP

5

"Will it shrink?"

CHAPTER IX

Life Wasn't Meant To Be Easy 1968–1978

CHAPTER IX
Life Wasn't Meant To Be Easy 1968–1978

Favourite pastime

The economic downturn that became established in the early 1970s changed the mood of Australia from the euphoria of the boom years to a troubled uneasiness concerning the future. Since most experts themselves were unsure of the cure, or indeed even of the cause of the economic malaise, the feeling of uncertainty became widespread. Cartoonists responded by lashing out at all and sundry in the hope that some of the barbs would hit home.

Politically the period was fairly unstable, with six prime ministers and numerous elections following Menzies' retirement in 1966 after 17 years in office. Under Gough Whitlam, the Labor Party achieved victory in 1972 to establish the first federal Labor government for 23 years, but lost in 1975 when Governor-General Kerr dissolved both houses and the Liberal Party was returned with an increased majority at the ensuing elections.

The social milieu of the times was exciting and despite the economic situation there was much evidence that Australians were undergoing a cultural renaissance of sorts. Writers, artists, poets and film-makers received a boost from government grants and were given a place to display their work when the Opera House was finally opened in October 1973. The women's movement, which made a big impact in the early 1970s with the publication of Germaine Greer's book *The Female Eunuch*, worked steadily over the years to improve the status and conditions of women in Australia. The Australian troops were brought home from Vietnam, and American soldiers on R and R disappeared from Sydney's Kings Cross. The conservation movement gained strength, with uranium mining the most contentious issue in recent times. The Report of the Commission on Human Relationships under Justice Elizabeth Evatt raised a storm of controversy when it was released in 1977. Aborigines and migrants began to defend their interests more effectively when they formed themselves into various political lobby groups, and in 1971, Neville Bonner became the first Aboriginal to be elected to parliament.

Trade unions were a popular target during this period. It was felt that their demands gave little reference to either international inflation, which had been precipitated by the 1973 rise in oil prices, or to the balance of world trade that had turned against Australia. Unions had grown in size and influence and, if public opinion polls were correct, many Australians believed that they wielded more power than any other group in society, including the government. In gaining shorter hours, more holidays, better working conditions and higher wages the unions had, according to their critics, weakened national productivity and damaged the country's previously favourable trading advantage to such an extent that some industries moved overseas.

Unemployment was a constant theme as the number of jobless rose from several thousands to hundreds of thousands. Continuing inflation also preoccupied the artists who conjured up a series of monsters to represent this ogre. It seemed that neither Liberal nor Labor governments could cope with an economy that now sank to depths previously only witnessed during the 1930s. Increasing drug abuse, crimes of violence and police corruption did little to alleviate the gloomy picture.

The daily newspapers maintained their monopoly over cartooning talent during the decade. The *Australian*, with Bruce Petty and then Larry Pickering, held the leading position in cartooning until the Melbourne *Age* took over through its promotion of such artists as Les Tanner, Arthur Horner, Bruce Petty (who had transferred in 1977) Ron Tandberg, Peter Nicholson and John Spooner, the caricaturist. The veterans continued on other papers, and newcomers joined the field in droves to confirm that Australia was in the forefront in the art of cartooning. The first female cartoonists (Roberto, Toone, Peyser, Leunig and Coopes) arrived on the scene.

Having obtained the good things in life on a platter for so long, Australians were conditioned to expect things to come easily. The representative figure of this period became the fat, beer-drinking ocker shown on this page. Gone forever were the lean and lanky figures that once stood for Australia.

These, then, were the concerns of the perplexed cartoonists, just as they were for the country's Prime Minister, Malcolm Fraser, who gave the period its cliché—*Life Wasn't Meant To Be Easy*.

The old and the new

1970–1977
Economic Nightmare

Within twenty years of the record 1951 wool export earnings, the price of the Australian staple had sunk to the lowest level for a quarter of a century. Beef prices began to fall, the nickel share boom inspired by Poseidon crashed, and the balance of world trade turned against Australia. Industrial unrest, unemployment and 'dole bludging' became the order of the day, crippling production and aggravating the already low productivity in the nation which only a decade before had earned the name of 'the lucky country'.

1 *"Think how worried we'd be"* (McCrae, *Courier Mail*, 1970). Bad seasons contributed to the fall in wool prices and helped to precipitate the recession of the early 1970s.

2 *"Handout . . . ?"* (Cedric, *Australasian Post*, 1976). Beef prices were so low that cattlemen were forced to shoot beasts to save on the cost of feeding them.

3 *"I thought to myself"* (Moir, *Bulletin*, 1976). The Poseidon scandal rocked the stock market and the business world when share prices plunged and many lost their investments.

4 *"Gee . . ."* (Atchison, Adelaide *Advertiser*, 1974). The unsuspecting and innocent citizen is alternately bludgeoned by inflation and unemployment.

5 *It's the first anniversary* (Tandberg, *Age*, 1977). Unemployment had brought hardship to hundreds of thousands as Australia faced its worst economic crisis for decades.

6 *"One lump or two?"* (Mitchell, *West Australian*, 1977). Inflation soared to double figures in the 1970s and remained there for some years.

7 *"A Shorter Week"* (Jeff, Melbourne *Sun*, 1976). Many blamed the unions for causing the economic recession.

1

"Think how worried we'd be if we had any sheep to shear!"

2

★ "HANDOUT . . .? Listen, mate; by the time he'd finished crying I'd slipped HIM a couple of dollars!"

3

"I thought to myself, maybe it's trying to tell us something."

4

"Gee . . . this is a tough neighborhood . . ."

5

6

"One lump or two?"

7

"A SHORTER WEEK WOULD BE NICE - YOU'D HAVE LESS TIME FOR STRIKE.

1968–1977
Running to Fat

The health of the community began to degenerate as the 'soft society' of the 1970s unfolded. More than twenty-five per cent of the population was suffering from obesity by 1976; cardiovascular diseases were killing 56 000 a year; cancer of various sorts claimed 20 000 annually, including 6 000 from cancer of the digestive system and 3 000 from cancer of the lungs; one in six suffered from high blood pressure; one in seven deaths was due to a stroke and life expectancy had come down to 67 years. Many blamed the unhealthy diet, others thought smoking and pollution were responsible and still others criticized the sedentary lifestyle of the soft society. Supposed to be a vigorous and healthy nation with plenty of opportunity for outdoor activities, Australia was fast becoming afflicted with all the health problems of the modern affluent society.

1 *Thank you for not smoking* (Leunig, *Nation Review*, 1977). Lung cancer claimed the lives of 3 000 Australians a year in the seventies.

2 *"I'm afraid"* (Berto, *Sun*, 1977). In an effort to counter the increasing obesity, many people joined 'weight-watchers' organizations.

3 *"It may look unhealthy"* (Langoulant, Perth *Daily News*, 1975). The average daily diet of Australians contains 1 000 calories in excess of requirements for a healthy life.

4 *"Compo"* (Mitchell, Adelaide *News*, 1976). Ever ready to attack complacency, cartoonists warned of the dangers of the 'soft society' that has begun to emerge in recent times.

5 *"So What . . ."* (Bateup, *Bulletin*, 1968). Sydney doctors performed Australia's first heart transplant in 1968.

6 *Canary* (Toone, *National Times*, 1977). Not only were Australians paying more for their medicine, but their pets were also costing them more in veterinary bills.

1

2

"I'm afraid I'll have to hang up — it's lunchtime already."

3

"It may look unhealthy to you, but in fact we're packed with natural goodness."

4

"Compo, sick leave, public holidays, bonuses, amenities! The inactivity is affecting my health . . . call Medibank!"

5

56,000 DEATHS IN AUSTRALIA PER YEAR DUE TO CARDIOVASCULAR DISEASE

NATIONAL HEART FOUNDATION OF AUSTRALIA

"SO WHAT ..... I'LL HAVE A TRANSPLANT"

6

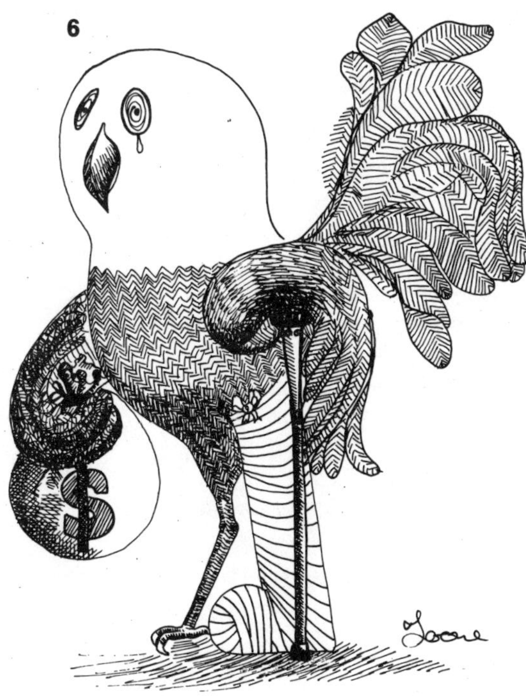

1964–1977
Soft in the Head

Education entered a crisis as funds, eroded by inflation, fell far short of the level needed to cope with an expanding population. Massive injections of finance were made in 1971 by the federal government and more money was requested following a senate report in 1972. The Karmel Report in 1973 asking for an immediate grant of $700 million to be shared between government and non-government schools served to aggravate the State-aid dispute. Not that this seemed important to those who believed there was little point in getting an education when it could not guarantee a job.

1 *One Of The Most Under-Developed Areas* (Petty, *Australian*, 1964). The education budget had been inadequate for years so when the economic crisis struck, the schools were worse off than ever.

2 *Where Are We Going?* (Tandberg, *Age*, 1977). With record unemployment Australia developed a surplus of highly qualified graduates.

3 *Do You Want A Generation?* (Cook, *Financial Review*, 1977). The special financial assistance granted to private schools angered some sections of the population.

4 *University Education* (Bateup, *Bulletin*, 1967). Many blamed the rivalry and confusion of role between federal and State authorities for the shortcomings in tertiary education.

5 *The old school tie* (Nicholson, *Age*, 1977). Some argued that because the needs of government schools were so pressing private schools should not have been given so much assistance in education budgets.

6 *Help* (Spooner, *Age*, 1974). Without adequate funding the educationists claimed they could not keep their heads above water.

1

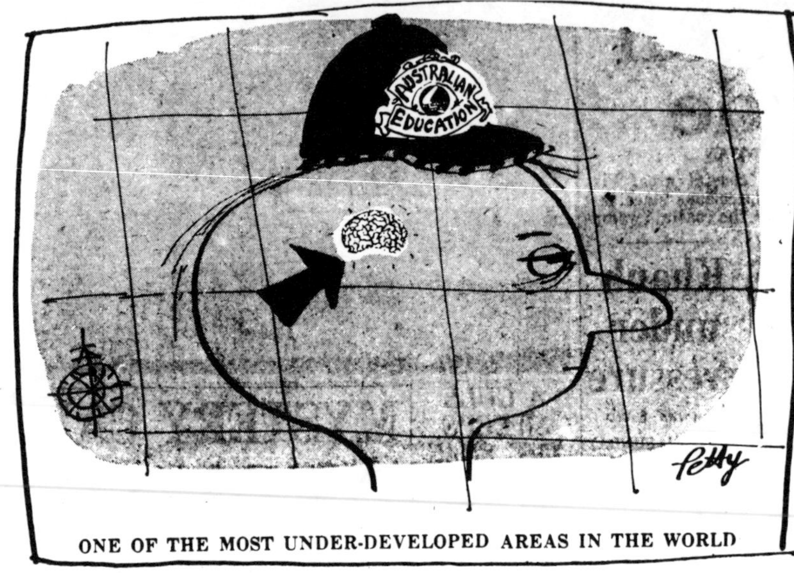

ONE OF THE MOST UNDER-DEVELOPED AREAS IN THE WORLD

2

3

4

STATE
UNIVERSITY EDUCATION
COMMONWEALTH.

5

GOVERNMENT SCHOOLS
CABINET
PRIVATE SCHOOLS
The old school tie

6

HELP
J.SPOONER

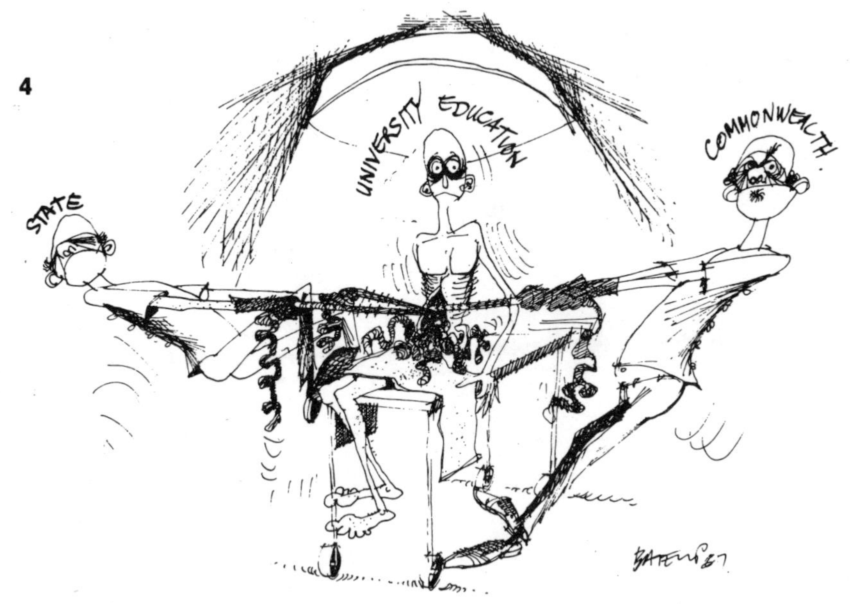

1970–1978
Kulcha for Vultures

The economic recession of the 1970s affected the arts considerably, although there were subsidies and grants on a greater scale during the years of the Labor administration. Financial support was generally lacking and this restricted theatre, film-making, writing and other cultural pursuits. A report by the Industries Assistance Commission in 1976 recommended the phasing out of all government subsidies to the arts over five years to minimize wastage in such non-profitable areas as opera and ballet. Matters were made worse when the ABC suffered heavy cuts in 1976 and 1977.

1 *Why's She Standing?* (Kev, Hobart *Mercury*, 1976). Despite the economic problems of the day large sums of money were paid for some works of art during the Labor government.

2 *"Get your gear off"* (Pete, Brisbane *Sunday Mail*, 1970). Theatre grew more avant garde during the period, with the production of 'Hair' presenting full frontal nudity on Australian stages for the first time.

3 *"Great Bandsman"* (King, *Sunday Telegraph*, 1976). Sometimes three national anthems were played on ceremonial occasions in 1976 and 1977 because the country at that time had still not agreed on the official version.

4 *The Occasional Grant* (Peyser, *Nation Review*, 1978). Australian writers eked out a precarious existence even under the grants schemes expanded by the Labor government.

1

2

3

'GREAT BANDSMAN O'GALLAGAN, HE CAN PLAY ALL FOUR ANTHEMS AT ONCE.'

4

1966–1977
The Rising of the Greenies

The conservation movement rose to a peak in the early 1970s when green bans were imposed by unions on many projects that threatened the environment. With the deepening recession however the union movement lost momentum, as its members were forced to put jobs before principles. Many other environment groups, however, grew and multiplied. The uranium debate generated much controversy after the publication of the two-part Ranger Uranium Environmental Inquiry, or the Fox reports as they were commonly called, in 1976 and 1977.

1 *"All this"* (Molnar, *Sydney Morning Herald*, 1966). The size of the city parks shrank in deference to progress.

2 *Election Issue* (Horner, *Age*, 1977). Many regretted Australia's decision to mine uranium, fearing it would turn the country into a wasteland.

3 *I Believe* (Collette, Melbourne *Herald*, 1976). Pollution, which appeared in Australian cartoons last century, had become a major theme by the mid-1970s.

4 *"Lightly the breath"* (Langoulant, Perth *Daily News*, 1975). Despite the Keep Australia Beautiful campaign, Australians continued to pollute their country with litter.

5 *This Is The Dawning* (Collette, *Australian*, 1971). The hazards of surfing on Sydney's beaches were suddenly increased with pollution.

1

'All this is public park, Madam. You can recognize it from the bench.

2

ELECTION ISSUE

3

4

"Lightly the breath of the spring wind blows; Though laden with faint perfume; 'Tis the fragrance rare that the bushman knows; The scent of the wattle bloom."

5

1972–1977
Quo Vadis?

Roads and transport have been the concern of cartoonists right from the early days of settlement. Crucial to the development of Australia has been the opening up of the country by roads and railways. These, however, have been sorely neglected with the advent of cheap air travel, which can reduce a three-day journey by road to a matter of hours. Nevertheless, Australians have more cars per capita than many other developed nations and this, as the cartoons show, creates enormous problems within cities, where air pollution and congestion can make life a misery for pedestrian and driver alike.

1 *Reduce Speed Now* (Pickering, *Australian*, 1976). The outdated 'highways' proved unable to cope with the increased traffic during the 1970s, when public transport remained as good—or as bad—as it had ever been.

2 *"In our language"* (Harrigan, *Daily Telegraph*, 1977). The traffic lights were switched over to computer control to cope with the increased volume of vehicles in the city.

3 *Must Have Been* (Petty, *Mirror*, 1977). The death and decay of a city is portrayed in a prophetic glimpse into the future.

4 *Freeways* (Nicholson, *Age*, 1977). Opposition to the freeways was strongest in Melbourne when, in 1977, more inner city areas were threatened with demolition.

5 *"Here he comes"* (Cav, Melbourne *Sunday Press*, 1977). A Melbourne group calling themselves Citizens Against Freeways barricaded new expressways to keep trucks from using them in 1977.

6 *"You Think It's Crook, Mate"* (Benier, *Daily Mirror*, 1976). Drivers are not the only ones to have problems with the roads.

1

2

"In our language it means: 'The computer has made a boo-boo'."

3

"Must have been quite a city before the traffic finally seized!"

4

THE CITY

FREEWAYS ...

"HERE HE COMES AGAIN — EVEL UPHEAVAL !!"

6

"YOU THINK IT'S CROOK, MATE — YOU OUGHT TO TRY PAINTING THE WHITE LINES DOWN THE MIDDLE ..."

1969–1978
Win a Few: Lose a Few

Once known as a 'nation of sportsmen', Australians began to suffer a few setbacks on the playing fields during the 1970s. In 1970–71 they lost the Ashes for the first time in twelve years. Sporting morale was further lowered when the America's Cup was then lost for the third time, Lionel Rose lost his world bantamweight title and Evonne Goolagong lost her Wimbledon title. Swimmer Shane Gould picked up three gold medals at the 1972 Munich Olympics but then in the 1976 Montreal Olympics Australia won no gold medals at all. The controversial cricket team formed by entrepreneur Kerry Packer then caused the weakened Australian Eleven to lose its first Test Match to India on Australian soil in 1978.

1 *"They're Gonna Ruin"* (Jeff, Melbourne *Sun*, 1975). There was controversy over whether spectators should be allowed to drink in certain areas of the cricket grounds.

2 *"Wake up Everybody"* Rigby, Adelaide *Advertiser*, 1963). Cricket hit a dull patch during the 1960s when the popular call was for 'brighter cricket'.

3 *'Spoil-sports!'* (Weg, Melbourne *Herald*, 1966). New regulations attempted to improve Australian Rules football and cut down on casualties.

4 *"In You Go"* (Lennon, Brisbane *Telegraph*, 1976). In its bid to host the 1982 Commonwealth Games, Brisbane is demonstrating that it would have more than adequate facilities.

5 *C'mon, John* (Peter, Melbourne *Truth*, 1977). Cricket became a more exciting game when fast bowler Dennis Lillee burst into the Test scene in 1972.

1

"THEY'RE GONNA RUIN CRICKET AS A SPECTACLE WITH ALL THESE DRY AREAS!"

2

"Wake up everybody—the mob on the Hill have picked up a couple of sides."

3

'Spoil-sports! It'll take all the FUN out of the game . . .

4

"IN YOU GO WE CAN ACCOMMODATE 400 OF YOU ATHLETES DOWN THERE."

5

1973–1977
Vive la Difference

The economic pressures of the day exacerbated the divisions in society and provoked a spate of cartoons about migrants and other minority groups. By 1970, Australia had received two and a half million migrants since World War II, yet the treatment of these 'New Australians' left much to be desired. The immigration programme was criticized for its racial selectivity and the government was urged by other countries to accept the refugees from Asia who began arriving by the boat-load in the second half of the 1970s. However, with a population in which a large proportion of people were born overseas or derived from European and other stock, Australia was becoming more tolerant of its migrants and minority groups although racism—and sexism—still prevailed.

1 *"All we were after"* (Tanner, *Age*, 1977). Vietnamese refugees caused acute embarrassment when they arrived in Darwin seeking asylum.

2 *It's a hard country* (Hobson, *Canberra Times*, 1977). With not enough jobs for Australians it was inevitable that the Vietnamese refugees would be resisted by many.

3 *"Come now"* (Logos, *Canberra Times*, 1973). Even though millions had arrived since World War II, migrants remained unsuccessful in their attempts to establish basic rights enjoyed by their counterparts in America.

4 *Immigration Dept Queue* (Cook, *National Times*, 1977). Although the dictation test had been replaced by an entry permit in 1958 the immigration policies nevertheless remained racist.

5 *To Prosperity* (Emeric, *Sun–Herald*, 1976). The budget vote for Aborigines was slashed by $33 million in 1976.

1

"All we were after were your hearts and minds — not your bodies".

2

3
Bill of Rights
MIGRANT RIGHTS
4
AUSTRALIANS
WOGS
REFFOS
CHOWS
SEPTICS
COONS
ETC
IMMIGRATION DEPT
QUEUE
5
TO PROSPERITY
BUDGET 76
emeric
22.8.76

1960–1977
Whatever Turns You On

Both drinking and drug-taking began to increase rapidly during the late 1960s and early 1970s. By 1976 Australians were averaging two 200 millilitre glasses of beer per head a day. Eighty-three per cent of men and 64 per cent of women admitted to drinking on a regular basis. During the period the per capita consumption of beer doubled. Drug-taking also increased to such an extent that a 1971 Senate report called for emergency legislation to halt the traffic. Drug-taking proved difficult to check however because of the difficulty of policing the coastline and of checking all incoming passengers on planes and ships.

1 *"Old Bert"* (Maynard, *Australasian Post*, 1960). The outback pub fulfilled both physical and social needs.

2 *"They say they're here"* (Moir, *Bulletin*, 1977). The town of Griffith was reputed to be the marijuana-growing capital of Australia.

3 *They Said* (Lodge, *Australian*, 1975). Drinking and smoking had become entrenched social habits by the 1970s and campaigns to check either met with great resistance.

4 *"It's all right, Dad"* (Molnar, *Sydney Morning Herald*, 1977). The greatest increase in marijuana usage in the 1970s was among schoolchildren.

5 *TV Repairs* (Neil, *Sun News Pictorial*, 1977). Watching television produced its occupational hazards as children were turned into 'vidiots'.

6 *"We thought"* (Pickering, *Australian*, 1976). Television was likened to a drug during the period as many viewers seemingly became addicted to it.

7 *". . . And to you"* (Fielding, *Northern Territory News*, 1977). People in the Northern Territory established a nationwide reputation as great beer drinkers.

1

★ **"OLD Bert shouldn't be dyin' of thirst . . . he only left 'ere an hour ago."**

2

"They say they're here for a wildflower tour around Griffith . . .!"

3

4

"It's all right, Dad. It's only pot."

5

TV REPAIRS

TODAYS CHILDREN VIDIOTS

HE HASN'T BEEN FEELING WELL LATELY....

Neil

6

7

" . . . AND TO YOU, OCKER OF DARWIN, THE COMPANION OF THE ORDER OF THE PIG."

1976–1978 Love at the Crossroads

The changing moral standards of the period were reflected in the increasing number of marriage breakdowns and record divorce statistics. The 1974–6 Royal Commission on Human Relationships headed by Justice Evatt reported a marked increase in the incidence of marriage failure and blamed this on an increasing materialism that had withdrawn attention from more fundamental human needs. The liberalization of the divorce procedures during the mid-1970s and the cheaper 'do-it-yourself' divorce kits obtainable by mail made it easier for uncontested cases to be settled. Nevertheless, despite the increasing divorce rates, statistics showed that a high percentage of divorcees were likely to marry again, and quite likely to seek the services of the growing number of civil celebrants.

1 *. . . and now let us pray* (Leunig, *Nation Review*, 1976). The hypocrisy of a religion that preaches charity and wishes for material goods is satirized.

2 *China* (Nicholson, *Age*, 1976). An earthquake struck China during the visit of Labor leader Gough Whitlam and his wife Margaret.

3 *"Hard to believe"* (Atchison, Adelaide *Advertiser*, 1977). The inequality of marriage partners contributed in many cases to marriage breakdowns.

4 *Your Erroneous Zones* (Roberts, *Nation Review*, 1977). Private fantasies are explored in mass marketed literature.

5 *Bar Scene* (Coopes, *National Times*, 1977). A gorilla sits at the bar while male drinkers stare at a female interloper.

6 *"No provisional licences yet . . ."* (Mitchell, Adelaide *News*, 1976). No longer 'til death us do part', marriage became a temporary arrangement as divorce figures soared.

. . . the Whitlams and the Chinese earthquake.

"Hard to believe that this could happen in Australia . . ."

5

6

"No provisional licences yet . . . but we're working on it!"

1972–1977
National Disasters

Misfortune struck often during the period when both natural and human-caused disasters have claimed increasingly large tolls. The collapse of Melbourne's Westgate Bridge in 1970; the Queensland floods early in 1974; the cyclone that destroyed much of Darwin on Christmas Day the same year; the collision that caused the fall of the Hobart Bridge in 1975 and the 1977 Granville train crash in New South Wales all sent shock waves around Australia. Patterns of violence seemed to be increasing at the same time, especially in Melbourne where in 1977 there was a record 350 bank robberies.

1 *Faulty Construction* (Petty, *Australian*, 1972). The collapse of Melbourne's Westgate Bridge claimed the lives of 33 workmen.

2 *Australia's Day* (McCrae, *Courier Mail*, 1974). Thirteen people died in the floods that crippled Queensland in January and February 1974.

3 *Dunkirk—1975* (Kev, Hobart *Mercury*, 1975). Ten people died when the cargo ship, the *Lake Illawarra*, brought down a span of Hobart's Tasman Bridge in 1975.

4 *"Is It Easier?"* (Neil, Melbourne *Sun*, 1977). Eighty-three people died in the 1977 Granville train disaster—the highest death toll in any accident in the history of Australia.

5 *Child Hanging* (Mary Leunig, *Nation Review*, 1977). New patterns of misfortune in the home emerged to baffle psychologists during the 1970s.

1

2

Australia's Day — Queensland's Hour

3

They were stranded. The news had told them the bridge was down. They we to the Bellerive Wharf. They were there — the little fleet. And they were ferri across — for nothing. The big job was to get people moving. The argui about what it would cost was something for later. Some people had said could happen . . . it had. It was Hobart's Dunkirk.

4

" IS IT EASIER TO BURY YOUNG BODIES THAN AN ANTIQUATED SYSTEM ? "

5

1975–1977
Fancy Fashions: Nothing Left!

Fashion trends were fast and furious during the 1970s and very few lasting preferences were established. Styles varied between generations, but there was a shared cosmopolitanism that had been lacking in past generations. The introduction of exotic clothes using eastern fabrics and designs reflected greater contact with Asian cultures. Jeans maintained their hold on the young, whose only other keynote was informality. The mini-skirt remained but became insignificant as women removed their bras and both men and women stepped out of costumes altogether on the beaches.

1 *Hi there* (Cook, *National Times*, 1976). Hippie fashions were a law unto themselves.

2 *Wage increases* (Mitchell, *West Australian*, 1970). The mini-skirt which had shocked people in the mid-1960s had been accepted by the 1970s.

3 *I would have signed* (Tandberg, *Age*, 1977). The pressure for legally approved nude beaches grew until State governments were forced to yield to the inevitable.

4 *"You see doctor"* (Langoulant, Perth *Daily News*, 1975). Unisex was in part an outgrowth of the feminist movement's aim of minimizing sexual exploitation.

5 *"No revealing blouse"* (Benier, *Mirror*, 1974). The Public Service fought a losing battle with the inevitable trends of the age.

6 *Don't look now* (Langoulant, Perth *Daily News*, 1975). Despite early battles with police, Australia boasted many nude beaches by the end of the period.

1

Hi there, I waved at you at Nimbin, but you didnt see me

2

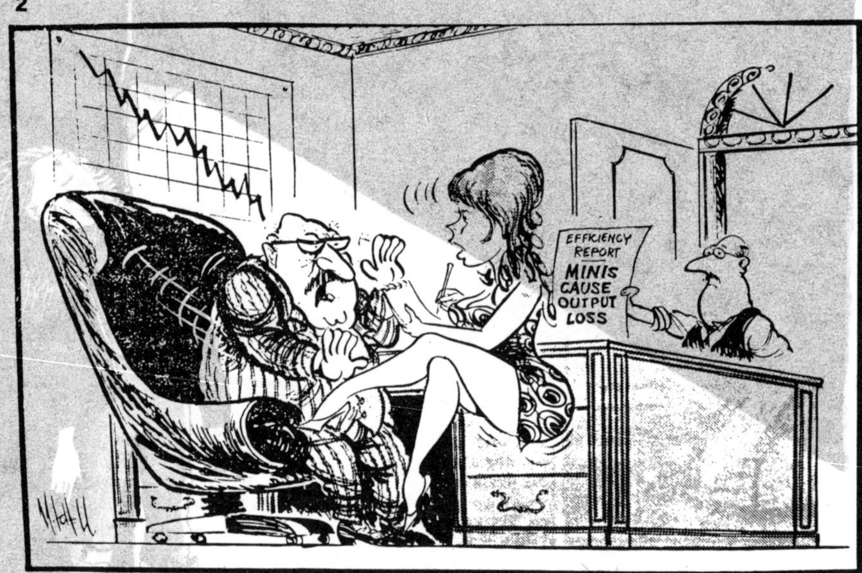

"Wage increases, credit squeezes, cost spirals—and now my own secretary stabs me in the back!"

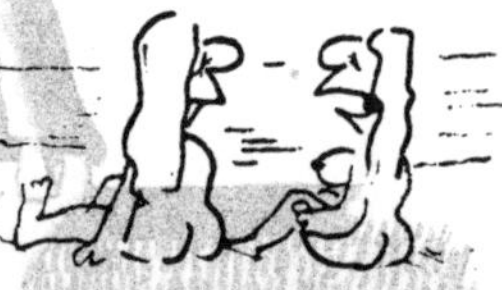

3

4

"You see doctor, my love person and I are worried about our child people's adjustment to a male-dominated society."

5

"NO REVEALING BLOUSE, NO SKIRT OF EXAGGERATED BREVITY, NO THONGS, NO FADED JEANS... OK-BUT YOU'LL HAVE TO PUT A BAND-AID OVER THAT NAVEL, MISS RASHLEIGH..."

6

"Don't look now, but I think we've a couple of plainclothes men in our midst."

INDEX

INDEX

'YOU KNOW, NICE PLACE FOR A HOLIDAY BUT I WOUL